Seven Weeks
for the SOUL

Seven Weeks
for the SOUL

A Reflective Journey for Lent or

Other Times of Renewal

Gerard W. Hughes

LOYOLAPRESS.

CHICAGO

LOYOLAPRESS.

3441 N. ASHLAND AVENUE
CHICAGO, ILLINOIS 60657

First edition 1993
This edition 1996
Reprinted 1993

Interior design by Lisa Buckley

Library of Congress Cataloging-in-Publication Data
Hughes, Gerard W.
    [Oh God, why?]
    Seven weeks for the soul : a reflective journey for Lent or other
times of renewal / Gerard W. Hughes.
        p. cm.
    Originally published: Oh God, why? Oxford, England : Bible
Reading Fellowship, 1993.
    ISBN 0-8294-1511-4
    1. Lent—Prayer-books and devotions—English. 2. Devotional
calendars—Catholic Church. 3. Prayer—Catholic Church. I. Title.

BX2170.L4 H84 2001
780'.9436'13—dc21
                                                    00-048803

PRINTED IN THE UNITED STATES OF AMERICA
01 02 03 04 05 / 10 9 8 7 6 5 4 3 2 1

✦

TO JOE AND MARGARET

✦

contents

Preface

Think of the fish we used to eat free in Egypt, the cucumbers, melons, leeks, onions and garlic! Here we are wasting away, stripped of everything; there is nothing but manna for us to look at!

NUMBERS 11:5—6

FOR FORTY YEARS THE ISRAELITES GRUMBLED THEIR WAY through the wilderness into the Promised Land, dissatisfied not only with their diet and with their leader, Moses, but also with God, who was ultimately responsible. They decided to reject him and create a more biddable god, a golden calf!

This long and bruising passing over from slavery in Egypt to freedom in the Promised Land is celebrated every year during the Jewish feast of Passover. It is not just a commemoration of a past event but also a celebration of a present reality, for God, who welded the Hebrew people into a nation through the trials of the wilderness, is the God of "the now," the "eternal God." "For the mountains may depart, the hills be shaken, but my love for you will never leave you and my covenant of peace with you will never be shaken, says Yahweh who takes pity on you" (Isaiah 54:10).

Having reached the Promised Land in spite of their rebellious attitudes, the Hebrew people realized that life, even with lots of milk and honey (and no doubt with an abundance of leeks, cucumbers, and garlic), could still be nasty, brutish, and short, and that their deliverance from Egypt was only a part of God's promise, not its fulfillment. Once they were in the Promised Land, their trials continued: the kingdom divided, the people were exiled, and Jerusalem was devastated. Whatever trials the Jews have subsequently endured they interpret in the light of their liberation from Egypt. The same God is still with them, leading them through their wilderness as he led their ancestors through the desert into the Promised Land. Centuries later, Isaiah reminds the exiled people,

> Yes, people of Zion, you will live in Jerusalem and weep no more. He will be gracious to you when he hears your cry; when he hears he will answer. When the Lord has given you the bread of suffering and the water of distress, he who is your teacher will hide no longer, and you will see your teacher with your own eyes. Whether you turn to right or left, your ears will hear these words behind you, "This is the way, follow it." You will regard your silvered idols and gilded images as unclean. You will throw them away like the polluted things they are, shouting after them, "Good riddance!"
>
> ISAIAH 30:19–22

God is constantly bringing his people, in spite of their grumbles, out of slavery, through the wilderness, and into the Promised Land.

As Christians, we also celebrate the Passover journey. Our understanding of that journey helps us understand our own lives. We believe that in Jesus God has fulfilled his promise to lead us out of slavery and into the Promised Land. That promise, first made to the Hebrew people, is a promise for all peoples of all times and nations. In Jesus, God has so identified himself with us that whoever we are, what we do to one another we do also to him. God is, in St. Augustine's words, "Nearer to me than I am to myself." Jesus lived, suffered, died, and is risen again, but "the Spirit of him who raised Jesus from the dead is living in you" (Romans 8:11). For Christians, Jesus is the Passover. Our life is a journey with him, a journey through life till death. In death, life is changed, not ended, because when we die, as the Eucharistic prayer reminds us, "we shall see you, our God, as you are. We shall become like you and delight in you forever through Christ our Lord, from whom all good things come" (Roman Missal). Our life is a journey not only with Christ but also in him and a liberation from slavery into the freedom of God.

In this book, we will look at this notion of journey in an effort to understand the meaning of our own lives, our grumbles and discontent, our pain and sadness, our hopes and dreams.

Thoreau once wrote, "The masses of men lead lives of quiet desperation," and he must have meant women as well. All of us, believers and unbelievers alike, have to find some purpose in life. We may think our purpose is to "eat, drink, and be merry," to acquire as much as possible, or to know, love, and serve God. Whatever our purpose, we soon discover that circumstances thwart us most of the time. Those dedicated to eating and drinking soon suffer indigestion or worse and lose their merriment. The money getters either cannot get enough or go bankrupt. The fervently religious discover, as the Israelites did, that God is not very comfortable to live with and that he can seem profoundly deaf to and uncaring of his chosen ones. So we try to alter the circumstances: the eaters and drinkers try Alka Seltzer, health spas, or surgery; the money getters try to change or bend the rules to recoup their losses; and the believers either become atheists or, like the Israelites, fashion a god more to their own liking. But circumstances have an inexorable quality and defeat us in the end, so we continue living "lives of quiet desperation."

Once we begin to see our lives as a journey with Christ to God, who loves us with a love that goes beyond all our thinking and imagining, the frustrating journey of quiet desperation begins to change. The circumstances remain the same, but we interpret them differently. We begin to see them as the nudgings of a God who takes pity on us, urging us to change direction on our journey. In traditional terminology, this change of perception is called penance, or repentance. In Greek, the word is *metanoia*, and it means "change of heart."

Seven Weeks for the Soul was originally a Lenten book, subtitled *A Journey through Lent for Bruised Pilgrims.* That journey is symbolic of the journey through life, which begins at conception and continues until death.

There are times on the journey when we must get our bearings so that we can continue on our way less frustrated and more at peace, less grumpy and more content, less downcast and more joyful. This orientation helps to set us free from our self-imposed slavery, enabling us to live more fully and to discover the joy of God that Christ promised his followers.

My thanks to Brian McClorry, S.J., for his helpful corrections and suggestions, to Shelagh Brown of the Bible Reading Fellowship for her encouragement and editing, and to Ursula Burton and Michael Paterson, S.J., for their constructive comments. For the diagram and notes in chapter 4 I am indebted to Gerald O'Mahony's book, *Making Use of Our Moods* (Guildford, England: Eagle Books).

PART ONE

PRACTICES FOR RENEWAL

Ways of Using This Book

AS I WORKED ON *Seven Weeks for the Soul*, I REMEMBERED my own past attempts at praying daily from the Scriptures: I always set out with good intentions but then became unable to concentrate, my mind fragmenting into countless distractions before I lapsed into sleep. When I did manage to stay awake and make some kind of prayer, I often felt the activity was like riding a bicycle without a chain, for what I was doing in prayer seemed to have little connection to everyday life. For a long time, I thought I was unique in my inability to pray, a conviction confirmed by some sermons and books on the beauty, value, and necessity of prayer. Now I spend much of my time listening to people describe their own experience of prayer, and I realize that I am not unique: the majority of people have a similar experience, each person believing that everyone else can pray better than he or she can.

I decided that the book would need a short section on ways of praying and on the relationship between prayer and everyday life. This section grew in the writing and now forms a third of the book, serving as an outline of the spiritual journey in which all of us are always engaged, whether we want to be or not. This section will, I hope, help you to see that Scripture readings are not simply accounts of God's past actions and Israel's response to them but guides that enable us to recognize God's present action in us as well as our response. The God of Abraham, Isaac, and Jacob, the Father of our Lord, Jesus Christ, is the same God who now holds us in being and is drawing us to himself through the everyday circumstances of our lives, just as he guided Israel.

One of the most important actions in the Christian life is repentance, having a change of mind and heart. Reading a book cannot change our mind and heart any more than reading a map can take us to our destination, but reading can initiate a process of change that continues long after the content of the book is forgotten.

Our minds seem to be constructed in layers. We use the top layers, for example, in making phone calls: recalling the number, transferring it to the dial, and then quickly forgetting it. This layer is very useful for satisfying examiners, but the information can go in and out of this layer of our minds without noticeably affecting our inner life or ways of behaving. People who have photographic memories can store a wealth of information, yet they can keep this information so well insulated from the rest of their consciousness that it does not affect their behavior. For example, an expert on world hunger could reel off horrifying statistics without feeling any compassion for the victims or any inclination to work to change the economic structures that inflict such misery on millions.

What is true of world hunger statistics in this example

is also true of religious knowledge. It is unlikely, but possible, that someone could know the Bible by heart, as well as the Christian creeds and the works of all the commentators and theologians who have ever lived, yet keep that knowledge sealed in the top layers of the mind so that it did not affect them on an emotional level. It is possible to read this book, even to know it by heart, without being affected by it in the least. Repentance happens at another, deeper layer of the mind.

In the preface to his *Spiritual Exercises*, St. Ignatius of Loyola, a sixteenth-century Basque who founded the Jesuit Order, gives us a few instructions. He warns that the giver of the Exercises should always be brief in presenting and explaining passages for prayer because what we discover for ourselves is much more effective of change than what another tells us and also because "It is not much knowledge that fills and satisfies the soul, but the intimate understanding and relish of the truth." I hope that the first part of this book will enable the reader, when he or she prays each day, to gain from prayer an intimate understanding and relish of the truth that effects inner change.

Deeper layers of the mind are slower at assimilating knowledge and are usually more retentive, not only of factual knowledge but also, and especially, of emotional experience. Throughout our lives, but particularly in childhood, this emotional experience has a profound and lasting effect on how we perceive the world, how we relate to others, how we react in different circumstances, and what reactions we provoke. It is in these deeper layers of consciousness that real change occurs, and any change that occurs in us affects, in some way, the whole of creation. The Israelites' journey was from Egypt to Palestine.

Each of our journeys is different, but one route is common to us all. Some have described it as the longest and most difficult journey in the world, the journey from the top layer of our minds to our hearts, where God is waiting to welcome us. Repentance means change at these deeper layers of consciousness. So how can we use this book to get in touch with our deeper layers?

We cannot reach our deeper layers simply by an act of will. Like anything else worth doing, the journey from mind to heart takes time. But don't be disheartened: even two or three minutes a day are better than nothing.

FOR TWO-MINUTES-A-DAY PEOPLE

Before you begin the daily readings, read part 1, "Practices for Renewal."

Each day in this book begins with a line of Scripture references. The reflection that follows the readings is based on these references, but because it would take at least two minutes to find and read these texts, I suggest you skip ahead to the shortened version that is provided for you each day and read it along with the reflection and prayer. When you have finished, take a few seconds to ask yourself whether any word, phrase, or image in the readings caught your attention, however slightly, and then underline it or make note of it. Without forcing yourself, try to recall the word, phrase, or image during the day.

Having given many individual retreats, I have learned that the most important element in this two-minute method is noticing the word, phrase, or image that has caught our attention. The deeper layers of our minds are usually more intelligent and aware of our real needs than the top layer, and when the deeper layer spots something important, it tends to retain it in our memory and to register its importance in our feelings. When I meet with retreatants for the first time after giving them a passage or two of Scripture to pray on, I listen very carefully for any word, phrase, or image that has caught their attention and has affected their feelings. Almost invariably these words or images will recur like a thread guiding them through their lives, enlightening and encouraging them, and bringing them to a better understanding of God and of themselves. Just today, a man who made a retreat several months ago told me of the continuing effect in his life of two images that came to him on the first day of his retreat, images that have become like lifelines for him.

On the weekends, when you have more time, you may like to try the fifteen-minute method that is explained below.

FOR FIFTEEN-MINUTES-A-DAY PEOPLE

You may find it useful to read part 1, "Practices for Renewal," once before you start using *Seven Weeks for the Soul* on a daily basis.

It is not necessary for you to look up all the Scripture references that are given at the start of each day; they are given simply for those who would like fuller Scripture readings. A shortened version of these readings is provided in the text for each day.

Read the passage, several times if necessary, until you are familiar with it. Make note of any word, phrase, or image that catches your attention and focus on it. You do not have to attend to every word of the passage. If you pray in the early morning, try to read the Scripture passage and reflection through once on the previous evening, allowing your subconscious mind to work on the material while you sleep. This usually makes it easier to pray the next morning. Ways of praying from Scripture are described in detail in a later chapter.

Before you begin your prayer, decide how much time you are going to give to it and keep to that length of time, no matter how bored you may feel. It seems that during prayer, we either have to pass through a period of emptiness and dryness or through a period of agitation before we reach our deeper layers of consciousness. If each time this occurs we abandon prayer in the hope that things will improve later, we will never reach the deeper layers of consciousness where change occurs.

FOR MEMBERS OF WEEKLY DISCUSSION GROUPS

Many readers of this book may already belong to parish or home discussion groups. In this section I offer some general guidelines for group meetings that, if followed, can deepen each person's prayer and show the close connection between prayer and everyday life. At the end of each week I offer more specific suggestions. If you do not belong to such a group, I offer suggestions for starting your own.

It has been said that at the Final Judgment, God will say to the just, "Come, you whom my Father has blessed, take for your heritage the kingdom prepared for you since the foundation of the world." To the others he will say,

"Now split up into discussion groups!" Discussion groups are welcomed by some, but to others, perhaps to most of us, discussion groups are a form of torture. So my first suggestion is that your group meetings be listening, not discussion, groups.

Why do so many people find discussion groups unsatisfactory? Simply put, it is because we do not listen to one another. We may hear each other's words and possibly be able to repeat them, but we do not allow them to enter the deeper layers of our consciousness where change occurs. We fear change more than death, a truth confirmed by our readiness as a nation to defend ourselves with a system of nuclear defense that threatens our own existence as much as that of our enemies. Real listening demands openness and readiness to change—in other words, listening is a form of penance. Prayer is listening to God, but for the listening to God to be genuine it must also be a listening to others. In discussion groups we tend to listen only to ourselves, to inflict our views on others, and to repel any contrary opinions. If others do not accept our views, we then accuse them of not listening, our unspoken assumption being that our views are so obviously right that anyone who disagrees cannot have been listening. In light of these behaviors, listening to others in your group is a very fitting exercise.

Because most of us are used to exchanging ideas in our discussion groups, we might think that a group meeting that forbids arguing and theorizing would reduce us to silence.

If there is no discussion, what do you talk about?

The object of your weekly meetings should be to share with one another, insofar as you are willing, your own prayer experience during the previous week, what you felt during and after the prayer, and the words or thoughts, memories or images that occasioned these feelings. Obviously there will not be time for everyone to describe his or her own experience in detail. It is therefore useful to keep a brief record of your own prayer each day by jotting down the predominant words or thoughts, images or memories that linger after you pray.

When we are first introduced to this method of sharing, most of us shy away from it because we are not accustomed to communicating at the deeper layers of our consciousness where change occurs. We prefer to remain safely on the surface, where we exchange weather reports or discuss the ghastly state of the economy, the world, and our neighbors. A woman who was having serious difficulties with her husband sat him down and told him that they needed to talk. His idea of "talking" was to comment on the unusual number of sparrows that had appeared in the garden! It will not be easy at first to communicate at a deeper level than this; it will be much easier to avoid looking at your own experience while launching instead into a theoretical discussion. Theoretical discussion has its place, but it rarely leads to communication at the deeper layers of our consciousness and thus does not effect inner change.

In discussion we develop a hidden agenda: We might appear to be discussing, for example, the meaning of humility, but underneath the pious phrases we start trying to show our greater knowledge, or wider experience, or superiority in the practice of the virtue! If we can persevere, avoiding all theoretical discussion, we will soon discover the value of sharing, in that it begins to deepen our understanding of ourselves, of others, and of God. In listening to one another, we are also listening to God, who rewrites the gospel daily in the minds and hearts of each of us.

I once told a loquacious friend that she talked too much and thought too little, to which she replied, "How can I know what I think until I've heard myself say it?" This is true for all of us. By putting our experiences into words, we can begin to see a little more clearly what is going on in the complexity of our minds and hearts. Once we express our fears and anxieties, for example, they no longer have such a hold over us. When we are afflicted with sadness or grief, words can enable us to survive the pain and help us avoid being plunged into panic or depression. Putting into words the joy, delight, or peace that we feel allows these feelings to permeate the deeper layers of our consciousness and to affect us more deeply and lastingly.

We all suffer from not being listened to, and we damage others by our own unwillingness to listen to them, be it intentional or unintentional. Instead of listening to and entering into the pain of a person grieving over a loss, we preserve ourselves and offer advice: "Come on, now, be brave. You can't go around moping for the rest of your life. Pull yourself together and start living normally." This kind of advice, although it might be given with the best of intentions, can be cruel and destructive to the recipient, who will be able to come to terms with his or her loss only if allowed to experience it. To experience the loss fully, they must feel safe enough to express their pain without being judged weak for having such feelings or being urged to get rid of them.

In your group, when one member is speaking about his or her prayer experience, the others should listen without interrupting unless they need clarification of something that they don't understand. Contradiction has no place in this type of discourse. If I say, for example, that I have been thoroughly bored by most of the last week's Scripture readings and prayer periods and irritated by the rest of them, no one can contradict me, because these are descriptions of my own inner state, of which no one else in the group has direct experience. I may then try to explain why I felt bored or irritated by the readings. As I do this, I may begin to realize that I experienced other feelings besides boredom and irritation and see connections between what I felt in the prayer and what has been going on in my life outside the prayer times, in my work and in my relationships with others. If a group is really listening without interrupting, giving advice, or making judgments, whether verbally or nonverbally, the speaker feels safe and can explore more easily the tangle of his or her own mind and heart. It helps to build up this atmosphere of trust within the group by accepting from the beginning that whatever is said during the meetings is strictly confidential.

After someone has spoken, take a few moments of silence before the next person is invited to speak. The silence is a sign of reverence for the speaker, but it also allows what he or she has said to sink into the deeper layers of our own consciousness where our attitudes toward one another can begin to change.

When we listen to one another's prayer experience, we soon learn the very important lesson that no two people pray in the same way and that the same Scripture text can have a different personal message for each of us. This knowledge can set us free to pay more attention to our own experience. Until we listen to other people's prayer experience, most of us are convinced that everyone else prays well and with ease and that we are the only ones who suffer boredom and emptiness, the only ones afflicted with a mind that disintegrates into myriad distractions as soon as we attempt prayer. It is encouraging to know that most people who attempt to pray regularly are similarly afflicted.

More important than this encouragement is the trust that we begin to have in our own experience. Many of us have been taught to ignore our own perceptions and trust the "experts," not only in religious matters but also in every other human encounter. So we discount what is going on in us, pay it no attention, try to follow the prescriptions of the experts, fail most of the time, and consequently feel like failures. We surrender our freedom to those who claim to know, perhaps paying them large sums of money for their expertise, and ignore the wisdom that God gives us.

Listening to our own and other people's prayer experience encourages us to drink from our own wells, to listen to the Holy Spirit at work in each of us. There is no such thing as failure in prayer. If I feel bored, empty, or angry when I pray, this can be as much a sign that I am in touch with God as when I feel full of peace, joy, and delight in God's presence. Until we learn to listen to and accept our own experience, we are incapable of repentance, of a change of mind and heart. This is why attending a weekly group meeting is a good spiritual exercise.

Listening is perhaps the greatest service we can provide for one another, and as you will discover, this kind of listening soon begins to affect your own way of praying. Listening to others' prayer experience and describing your own to them makes you more attentive to what is going on within you. It is only by listening to ourselves that we can listen to God, who is "closer to me than I am to myself." We have no other option. That is why God says through the psalmist, "Be still, and know that I am God!" (Psalm 46:10, NRSV).

You should arrange your meetings so that after everyone has had the opportunity to speak, you have some time left to reflect together on what you have heard. During the reflection time, you can tell each other what has helped you in what you have heard. You should also use this time to discuss practical matters, to answer questions or address comments about books, articles, TV or radio programs, or conversations that you have had. God is the God of compassion. When the Spirit of God is at work in a group, then the spirit of compassion takes hold of the members, and they become more aware of the need to serve the community in which they are living.

It is also good to set aside time to silently pray for one another, whether at the beginning or at the end of your meetings. Perhaps you could sit in a circle around a lighted candle, a symbol of Christ, light of the world, who is in fact within and among each of you. It is important to pray in silence and resist breaking the silence with vocal prayer or singing.

If possible, ensure that your group is ecumenical. In *The Constitution of the Society of Jesus*, St. Ignatius wrote, "The more universal a work is, the more it is divine." Jesus prayed that we all might be one. By sharing our prayer experience with Christians of other denominations, we get a glimpse of the unifying work of God, come to appreciate the special gifts of other denominations, and experience the unity of Christ, which holds all things in being.

For each meeting, appoint someone to lead the group, a task that should be taken by each member in turn. The leader has only two functions: first, to ensure that each person who wants to speak has the chance to do so, and second, to ensure that each speaks out of his or her own experience and does not theorize about it. The entire group should share this responsibility with the leader.

If you do not belong to a group or if there is not one in your neighborhood, then you can start your own group with one or two other people. If the group is healthy, participation will affect not only the prayer life of its members but also every other aspect of their lives, and the group will begin to engage in some kind of common outreach.

Here are a few final practical points about group meetings:

- The ideal size for a group of this kind is six to eight people. If there are more, listening becomes exhausting. Healthy groups will increase and multiply.

- Decide at the first meeting what the starting and finishing times will be for each meeting and keep to them strictly.

- If possible, meet in a different member's home each week. If refreshments are offered, keep them simple, so that no one has to spend a lot of money.

Chapter 1

Why Prayer, Fasting, and Almsgiving?

AS I MENTIONED AT THE START OF THIS BOOK, *Seven Weeks for the Soul* was originally written as a Lenten book. Lent is the most unpopular time in the Christian year because it is a time for prayer, fasting, and almsgiving. In this chapter we will look briefly at the origins and development of Lent to see how important prayer, fasting, and almsgiving are for Christians today.

People have an unhealthy dislike of the body that predates Christianity. This distortion has lasted through centuries and has flourished at certain periods of church history in spite of official condemnation of the doctrine that the spirit is good and the body is evil. This dualistic doctrine has produced contrary results among its holders. Some have concluded that, as the body is evil, one cannot be held responsible for its behavior, so they let the body follow its inevitably evil ways while keeping the spirit pure. This is a convenient way of solving life's struggle by permitting the holder of the doctrine to practice base debauchery while retaining a sublime spirituality. This dualistic tendency is deeply rooted in human nature and survives in many forms, even in those that reject or are ignorant of the theory that spirit is good and matter is evil. I recently saw it in a three-year-old girl who was fiercely scolding and spanking her doll for being naughty. The naughtiness was the little girl's own, but she was obviously experiencing great relief in transferring it to the dolly while relishing her own righteousness. This same tendency remains with us throughout our lives, but later in life we substitute other human beings for the doll. Christianity teaches that our spirits, and not only our bodies, are inclined to evil. The French scientist and philosopher Pascal once wrote of a convent of Religious Sisters that they were "as pure as angels and as proud as demons."

Others interpret the dualistic doctrine to mean that the body, being evil, must be constantly opposed, punished, and kept under strict subjection. This conclusion, while less damaging to the public interest than the first, is hard on its holders because it condemns them to a life of misery. Yet in past ages, severe treatment of the body has often been considered an indicator of holiness, often in direct proportion to the bodily austerities practiced. The story of one saint's life describes his early signs of holiness: As a baby, he refused his mother's milk on Fridays. But this was only a hint of greater things to come. He went on to practice the fiercest austerities before dying, not surprisingly, at an early age.

The effects of holding this dualistic doctrine are still with us and can be witnessed daily, especially in city parks, where young and old jog with agonized expressions on their faces. I am not condemning jogging or physical fitness but only noting that our dislike of the body is manifest in countless ways. Slimming, dieting, and beautifying, like jogging, are good in themselves, but they can also be expressions of self-rejection, of dislike of our own bodies. Christian emphasis on self-denial can foster this spirit of self-rejection to the point that the body itself becomes a constant source of guilt and misery. The other extreme is to believe that care of the body equates to the whole of spirituality, so that having had my vegetarian meals, massage, and Jacuzzi, I am now ready to meet my Maker!

In Christian spirituality today, there is much less emphasis on self-denial and mortification. In his immensely popular book *Original Blessing*, Matthew Fox writes of the church's morbid preoccupation with original sin, which produces a guilt-ridden people by concentrating the Christian mind on sin and punishment instead of turning it to the goodness of God, manifest in creation and in our own body, mind, and spirit.

Should we not, then, scrap the season of Lent as a time for prayer, penance, fasting, and almsgiving and turn it into a time of celebration and thanksgiving—enjoying, appreciating, and relishing God's gifts instead of denying ourselves that enjoyment? Instead of deciding what to give up for Lent, should we not decide what we are going to enjoy and relish, making Lent a happier time for ourselves? Before you answer these questions, let's take a brief look at the origins and development of Lenten practice.

Healthy Christian spirituality has its roots in Judaism. The Jews hold a seven-day fast before the Passover, not in preparation for the feast but as part of the celebration.

Before the fast begins, all unleavened bread must be removed from the house. The unleavened bread, bitter herbs, and wine recall the anguish and the joy of the Israelites' rescue from Egyptian slavery. In Christianity, the fast is generally seen more as a preparation for Easter than as a participation in the Passover mystery, which can lead to the false conclusion that the Easter mystery begins on Easter Sunday.

Whether Lent is to be considered as a preparation for Easter or as participation in the mystery may seem to be an academic dilemma. It is, however, a very practical question that helps us understand not only Lent but all of our Christian celebrations and their relationship to everyday life and behavior.

In celebrating Easter, for example, we are not simply recalling Christ's resurrection of two thousand years ago but are celebrating the mystery of our own lives now. We are on a journey to a new life. Death is not the end but the beginning of a new phase, "when every tear will be wiped away and we shall see you, our God, as you are. We shall become like you and praise you forever through Christ, our Lord, through whom all good things come" (Eucharistic prayer, Roman Missal). Life is a journey into death, a journey out of slavery and into freedom, a journey made in hope. We celebrate Christ's resurrection to remind ourselves of our own destiny and that we are not alone in our journey through life. For Christ, who entered once into our humanity, our sinfulness, our suffering, and our death, is now out of time and therefore continuously present in every moment of our time—"Jesus Christ is the same today as he was yesterday and as he will be for ever" (Hebrews 13:8). We are on a journey to sharing his resurrection. We celebrate Lent to make ourselves more aware of the nature of the journey we are taking and to give ourselves direction and hope.

The first mention of Lent appears in a church document by the Council of Nicaea (A.D. 325). In early centuries, Christians probably followed the Jewish custom of praying and fasting for one week before the Passover. Lent as we know it began as a time of special preparation for new converts to Christianity, who were baptized on Holy Saturday. It also became a time for the reconciliation of those Christians who, in times of persecution, had denied their faith or had committed some other public crime, separating themselves from the church. The ceremony of reconciliation took place on Maundy Thursday. The official prayers and readings for Lent still depict Lent as a time of preparation for baptism and of reconciliation for public sinners, who began Lent by wearing ashes on their heads as a sign of repentance. Soon the practice of Lent was extended to the whole church, for we are all sinners and in need of repentance. Lent became a collective retreat within daily life for the whole church, a time for entering more consciously into the mystery of Christ's Passover from death to resurrection and for imitating Christ in his forty days in the desert, where he faced the devil's temptations. Jesus was "led by the Spirit out into the wilderness to be tempted" (Matthew 4:1). Lent was a time for fasting and meeting the demons, a time for spiritual battle.

Although "meeting the demons" and "spiritual battle" are unfamiliar terms to many Christians today, they were very familiar to fourth-century Christians. When the Roman Empire became officially Christian, the status of Christians changed. Clerics became state officials. Being a

Christian, formerly a risk to one's life, now became a mark of respectability. Many Christians, especially among the laity, were uneasy about the change. They saw the subtle dangers of this apparent victory and feared that imperial recognition would imperil the gospel message more effectively than imperial persecution had done. This concern drove thousands of Christians out of the cities and into the desert, where they believed the hidden forces of evil would be unmasked, stripped of their imperial plausibility, and overcome in spiritual battle. This Christian protest was the origin of the monastic movement, but it would be almost a hundred years before the official church would recognize its significance.

The Gospel readings for the first Sunday of Lent are always the accounts of Jesus' forty days in the desert. After his baptism by John, Jesus "was led by the Spirit out into the wilderness to be tempted by the devil. He fasted for forty days and forty nights, after which he was very hungry, and the tempter came . . . to him" (Matthew 4:1–3).

The devil's temptations are very subtle and are presented, with scriptural authority, as good and reasonable. The devil first suggests, "If you are the Son of God, tell these stones to turn into loaves" (Matthew 4:3). After all, God loves his creation; he is the God of generosity, the God of compassion, so why torture yourself? Why not satisfy your own hunger and the hunger of thousands of others? Why not experience the goodness of God for yourself and let others know it too? Then the devil takes Jesus up to the parapet of the temple in Jerusalem and suggests, "If you are the Son of God . . . throw yourself down; for Scripture says: 'He will put you in his angels' charge, and they will support you on their hands in case you hurt your foot against a stone'" (Matthew 4:6). This is also a very reasonable suggestion. Why not take a leap off the temple pinnacle, preferably when lots of people are around, for your safe landing will certainly convince them of your unique status and will thus encourage them to listen respectfully and obediently to your words of truth? Finally, the devil takes Jesus to a very high mountain and shows him all the kingdoms of the world and their splendor. The devil says, "I will give you all these . . . if you fall at my feet and worship me" (Matthew 4:9). Again he offers a reasonable suggestion. Why not take over all the powers and kingdoms of the world and use the power and wisdom to protect people from their own evil and destructive ways? If you do not take them over, then others will, and they will use that power to their own advantage. So why not prevent them, for their own good and the good of countless others?

In "The Grand Inquisitor" chapter of his novel *The Brothers Karamazov*, Fyodor Dostoyevsky imagines Christ's reappearance in Spain and his trial before the Inquisitor. In the fictional account, the Inquisitor condemns Jesus to death because Jesus gave all the wrong answers in the desert and is, consequently, undermining the church, whose vocation it is to save human beings from the destructive effects of their freedom. According to the Inquisitor, the church should be giving the people food to eat and miracles to strengthen their faith and should exercise its power to curb the people's destructive will.

In the temptations, Jesus uncovers the deceits of the Evil One because Jesus' whole being is at one with God: "You must worship the Lord your God, and serve him alone" (Matthew 4:10). Lent is a time for prayer, a time for unmasking the subtle and destructive forces masquerading as good in our own time, in our individual lives, in the life of the church and of the nation.

Lent is a time not only for prayer but also for fasting and almsdeeds. Augustine called fasting and almsdeeds "the wings of prayer," presumably meaning that without them our prayer remains earthbound and ineffective. This reasoning touches on a problem of our spirituality today that affects all Christian denominations, and its importance cannot be exaggerated.

The problem is that our spirituality is split: we have split God off from life. We worry about our dwindling numbers and near-empty churches and blame them on secular values and the permissiveness of our age, but increased numbers and packed churches would not necessarily solve the problem. Perhaps the dwindling numbers are a blessing, if we can use them to reflect on why so many good, generous, and intelligent people abandon the practice of formal religious worship.

En route to Jerusalem a few years ago, I visited Medjugorje, a village in what was then Yugoslavia. Our Lady was said to have been appearing daily to a group of children since 1981, declaring herself to be the Queen of Peace. Since then, millions of people have flocked there to pray. When I visited in May 1987, thousands of visitors from the United States, Europe, Ireland, and Britain were there praying for peace. Most of the people to whom I spoke were stout defenders of nuclear deterrence as a necessary policy for maintaining peace. They saw no inconsistency in holding these views while at the same time praying for peace. This illustrates the split in spirituality that, in the Roman Catholic Church, can be summed up as the split between the "Rosary Brigade" and the activists. The members of the "Rosary Brigade" believe that the most effective way of ensuring world peace is prayer, and the activists believe that without effective political and social action peace remains an abstract ideal. This same split runs through all the denominations: the charismatics versus the political and social activists, the evangelizers versus the community developers. I know that many Christians do both—pray and practice social and political activism—but they are not the majority, and they usually meet with fierce opposition from their own Christian brothers and sisters. The division has deep roots in our religious terms for "nature" and "grace"—natural and supernatural—terms that can easily be misunderstood as supporting the split. By not allowing God to be the God who became one of us in Jesus, this division keeps God at a safe distance from our everyday behavior and from our individual and national attitudes, values, and policies.

Here are three illustrations of our split spirituality.

1. No Christian is likely to cause uproar in a church by praying, "Lord, grant peace to our world." It is a safe prayer to make, allowing those who make it to continue pursuing peace by whatever means they think effective. Let us suppose, for example, that I, in company with all the political parties and the majority of Christians and Christian leaders, am a firm believer in our national defense policy as a means of preserving peace. Why then should I not make the following prayer for peace?

> Dear Lord, inspire our scientists that they may invent yet more lethal weaponry (since the more lethal it is, the more effectively it will deter), preserve us from any unfortunate accident in its testing (lest

we suffer an even greater disaster than Chernobyl),
and bless our economy that we may put these
weapons into plentiful production (or they will fail
to deter). Succor the homeless, the unemployed, the
sick, and the elderly of our own and other nations
until such time as our defense commitments allow
us to do more. Strengthen our leaders in a strong
defense policy, drive out from our midst any who
by thought, word, or deed undermine our national
security, and grant us the protection of nuclear
weaponry now and forever. Amen.

Some readers may dislike this prayer and consider it a
distortion of the views of those who find morality in policies
of nuclear deterrence. However, it does illustrate the split
nature of our spirituality—that when we bring our everyday
actions and attitudes into prayer, our prayers disturb.

2. Recently I met with a group of Christian psycho-
therapists, most of whose clients are also Christian.
I asked these therapists whether, in the course of their
therapy sessions, they ever asked their clients about their
prayer or encouraged them to pray over the questions
arising in their sessions. The therapists replied that they
did not and explained that if they encouraged their clients
to pray over their problems, their clients would use prayer
as an escape from facing their problems. I could accept
this answer, but I also saw it as a commentary on the split
nature of our spirituality—that prayer can be used as an
escape from the facts in which we are living.

3. This is an exercise that you can try for yourself.
Imagine your doorbell ringing one evening. When you
answer, you discover that the visitor is the risen Lord
himself. Somehow, you know it is the Lord. How do you

react? Do you shut the door on him or tell him to come back on Sunday? Presumably you welcome him in, summon everyone in the house, and find yourself making such ridiculous statements to the Lord of all creation as "Do make yourself at home and stay as long as you like. Everything is yours." Now imagine it is two weeks later. Jesus has accepted your invitation and he is still with you. Do you remember that disturbing passage in the Gospel where Jesus says, "It is not peace I have come to bring, but a sword. For I have come to set a man against his father, a daughter against her mother, a daughter-in-law against her mother-in-law" (Matthew 10:34–35)? The letter to the Hebrews says, "Jesus Christ is the same today as he was yesterday and as he will be for ever" (Hebrews 13:8). How are things at home now? Most likely there has been a bit of friction during family meals in the last two weeks, with some members leaving the table and slamming doors—possibly the front door, never to return again. You invited Jesus to make himself at home, so he has begun to invite his friends to your house. In the Gospel, people said that Jesus dined with sinners. What kind of people do you now see coming to your house? What are the neighbors saying, and what is happening to the local property values? Soon you decide that you must not keep Jesus all to yourself, so you arrange for him to give a talk at the local church. Do you remember that scene in the Gospel where he addresses the scribes, Pharisees, and chief priests and assures them that the criminals and the prostitutes will get into the kingdom of God before they do? He gives the same message to a gathering of men and women at St. Jude's parish, and the ensuing uproar results in the parish losing its principal benefactors.

You return home with Jesus, the savior who has now become your problem. What are you to do? You cannot throw out the Lord of all creation. So you look around the house, find a suitable cupboard, clear it out, decorate it sparing no expense, put a good, strong lock on it, and put Jesus inside. You place a lamp and flowers outside the cupboard, and each time you pass it you bow reverently so that you still have Jesus but he does not interfere with your life anymore!

This is an image that you can use in your own prayer and reflect on afterward.

Scripture is full of warnings against split spirituality, and most of the Scripture readings during Lent focused on this point. The Old Testament prophets fulminate against lip service to God and against religious worship that is not the true expression of the worshiper's heart and soul.

> I cannot endure festival and solemnity. Your New
> Moons and your pilgrimages I hate with all my
> soul. They lie heavy on me, I am tired of bearing
> them. When you stretch out your hands I turn my
> eyes away. You may multiply your prayers, I shall
> not listen. Your hands are covered with blood, wash,
> make yourselves clean. Take your wrongdoing out
> of my sight. Cease to do evil. Learn to do good,
> search for justice, help the oppressed, be just to the
> orphan, plead for the widow.
>
> ISAIAH 1:13–17

The practice of prayer alone is not sufficient to heal the split in our spirituality or to unmask the subtle deceits of the destructive spirit working within and among us. Nor will prayer alone enable us to recognize the creative action of God's Spirit, which is also working within and among us all. Therefore, the church insists that we fast and give alms if we want our prayer to be effective.

In early centuries the Lenten fast was very severe, allowing only one meal per day, toward evening, which could not include any meat or dairy products. In later centuries the discipline was relaxed; the main meal could be at noon and could include dairy products, and a light meal was allowed in the evening. The Roman Catholic Church, which used to be so precise in its rules and regulations, today imposes fasting only on Ash Wednesday and Good Friday and provides no detailed fasting prescriptions. Today, fasting is generally understood to mean eating only one main meal and two smaller meals in the day, a prescription that would be an undreamed-of luxury for millions of people.

A person may fast for a variety of reasons—to achieve a slimmer body, greater fitness, or better health, to save money, or out of necessity—reasons that are not necessarily spiritually motivated. A person may undertake general asceticism—the practice of self-denial and bodily austerity—for many different reasons that also bear no relation to penance. Adolf Hitler, for example, was a most abstemious man: a vegetarian, a nonsmoker, a teetotaler. Although fasting is often motivated by secular concerns, in Christian tradition, it has always been recommended. Why is this? Jeremiah writes "The heart is more devious than any other thing, perverse too: who can pierce its secrets?" (Jeremiah 17:9). Fasting can help us clear our minds so that we can recognize more quickly the deceits that operate within us. The physical effects of fasting vary from person to person, but for many, provided the fast is not too prolonged or severe, it has an energizing effect. Fasting enables us to feel more compassion for the millions who fast daily out of necessity; by sharing their hunger, we are more likely to respond to their need by contributing to aid organizations and finding out what we can do politically to alleviate the problem.

What form our fasting should take is for each one of us to decide. We will not do ourselves any harm by avoiding luxuries and junk food. Fasting is a means to an end, not an end in itself, so practice whatever form enables you to pray more regularly and wholeheartedly, but do not allow the fasting to become an endurance test or an ego trip.

Like prayer alone, fasting alone does not necessarily bring us nearer to God, and the prophets denounce fasting that does not spring from compassion and a hunger for justice.

> Fasting like yours today will never make your voice heard on high. . . . Is not this the sort of fast that pleases me—it is the Lord Yahweh who speaks—to break unjust fetters and undo the thongs of the yoke, to let the oppressed go free, and break every yoke, to share your bread with the hungry, and shelter the homeless poor, to clothe the man you see to be naked and not turn from your own kin?
>
> ISAIAH 58:4, 6–7

Fasting from wrongdoing is more important than fasting from food, but fasting from food can help us fast from wrongdoing, from oppressing our workmen, as Isaiah says, and from quarreling and squabbling.

We can also participate in an inner fasting of the mind, a fasting from walking along those dark inner paths of self-pity, from blaming others, from relishing the failures of others, from nursing grievances. Because we do have to walk those paths in our inner minds, it is important to develop a habit of thanking God for everything we have enjoyed in a day.

Almsgiving is an unfortunate word, for it implies a giving of the fortunate to the less fortunate, a giving that can humiliate the receivers, estrange them even more from their benefactors, and perpetuate an unjust system of haves and have-nots that never should have existed in the first place. Like fasting, almsgiving is both a means to helping us pray and the result of prayer. If our prayer is genuine, then the Spirit of God, the God of tenderness and compassion, will take hold of us, and we will begin to feel more at one with him and with creation. Our hearts, like Christ's, will be "moved with pity," and we will begin to feel for our neighbor as we feel for ourselves. *Almsgiving* is a generic term that expresses the practical nature of our love for others. We do not just pray and fast for them; we give them practical proof of our love. Almsgiving may take a variety of forms. It includes the corporal works of mercy—caring for the sick, the homeless, and the hungry—and this work too may take a variety of forms. In many cities, volunteers organize soup kitchens and night shelters for the homeless, which, although it is excellent work, may not be touching the root of the problem of hunger and homelessness. Instead, it may only be covering up the problem. Almsgiving means not only giving handouts but also addressing the root causes of hunger and homelessness. Almsgiving is less favored by

Christians because it may reveal the need for radical change in our own lifestyles, result in a loss of privilege and status, and lead us to a discovery of our own inner poverty. The Book of Revelation warns the people of Laodicea, "You say to yourself, 'I am rich, I have made a fortune, and have everything I want,' never realizing that you are wretchedly and pitiably poor, and blind and naked too" (Revelation 3:17).

Almsgiving includes not only the corporal works of mercy, at both the individual and the structural levels, but also what is, for most of us, a much more difficult giving—forgiving. Lent is a time of forgiveness from God and therefore also a time for our forgiveness of one another, a time for letting go of past resentments and breaking down the barriers that separate us.

Traditionally, Lent has been a time for prayer, fasting, and almsgiving. In Christianity we have emphasized original sin more than the original blessings of God, thus developing a spirituality that is suspicious of pleasure and presents God as disapproving of almost everything, and certainly of everything we like. It is right that we should turn away from such an appalling picture of God. Yet the prophets, Jesus, and all the spiritual teachers in the church have constantly advocated prayer, fasting, and almsgiving, and we would do well to heed this teaching. It is not our prayer and fasting that have given us this false image of a punishing God, but their neglect. Without prayer and love for our neighbor, this view of a forbidding God flourishes within us and within the church, to our own and everyone else's detriment.

Chapter 2

The Meaning of Penance

THE WORDS *penance* AND *penitence* ARE NO LONGER FASHION-ABLE in religious circles and have been replaced by the word *renewal.* Countless courses promising to renew us individually and corporately are offered in the churches, and while participants in such courses may be very satisfied with them, outside observers have not seen an enlivening of church services, increased attendance, or any obvious benefit to those outside the renewal group.

It is always risky when Christians attempt to renew, reform, or convert themselves, and the more they appear to succeed, the greater the danger. Renewal, if it aims at self- or group improvement, will probably do far more harm than good to the individual, group, and society around them. This sweeping statement, while it may seem a cynical and unjust condemnation of many sincere individuals and groups within the church, is made simply to point out that the more we try to be "good" Christians, the more we are bound to fail. When we fail, we feel demoralized, confirmed in our own feelings of uselessness and failure, and surrender our lives to feelings of inferiority. If we do succeed, our egos are boosted and become our greatest obstacles to finding God. Of the two alternatives, the former is probably safer, because we are normally closer to God when we feel inadequate than when we feel complacent. In the Gospels, Jesus never condemns the dispirited, but he is vitriolic in his condemnation of those who claim to have a monopoly on God.

Our renewal, like our good resolutions, is always doomed to fail as long as the focus is on self-improvement. All Christian renewal, if it is to bring about a real change of mind and heart, must start not from effort but from attentiveness to God, who alone is good. We pay lip service to this truth in so many of our renewal attempts, praying for God's blessing on our endeavors and then concentrating our minds on the latest technique for self-betterment. We try so hard to make our prayer successful that we leave no room for God to pray in us: "Pause a while and know that I am God" (Psalm 46:10).

All the great feasts of the church—Easter, Pentecost, and Christmas—are celebrated not primarily to remind us of past events but to help us understand, appreciate, and relish the mystery of our present existence. Jesus is not born again every Christmas. He does not rise every Easter Sunday, nor does the Holy Spirit appear like a dove every Pentecost. In an ancient homily that appears in the Roman Office readings for Holy Saturday, the anonymous author imagines Jesus going down to hell after his death, knocking on the door, and summoning Adam. Their conversation ends with the astonishing sentence, "Adam, arise, come forth. For henceforth you and I are one undivided person!" God is calling you and me to arise and live in this way. This is the meaning of the call to repentance.

A friend of mine came to see me after attending a meeting in which all present had to introduce themselves to one another. They were asked to identify themselves first with their names, then with their occupations. When it came to my friend's turn he wanted to say, "I am Donald. I am a unique manifestation of God."

We become so absorbed in the details of our religion that we lose sight of the astonishing truths on which it is all based. Each one of us is a unique manifestation of God, who is "closer to me than I am to myself." Jesus said of his relationship to us, "I am the vine, you are the branches" (John 15:5), and he prayed "may they be one in us, as you are in me and I am in you . . . that they may be one as we are one" (John 17:21–22). And Paul says that even before the world began God had us in mind: "Before the world was made, he chose us, chose us in Christ, to be holy and spotless, and to live through love in his presence" (Ephesians 1:4). Our faith is certainly not lacking in wonderful statements; the problem is appropriating those statements, making them real to ourselves, and really believing them instead of just piously mouthing them. What an enormous difference it would make in our lives if we believed that our ultimate identity is in God, that each of us is one undivided person with Christ. If we had that conviction, then when we were insulted, criticized, or overlooked, we could remain unperturbed, even grateful for the criticism. Similarly, we would not be shattered if we lost what wealth we had or our jobs.

If statements like "our ultimate identity is in God" seem abstract to us, it is helpful to set aside our conscious minds and ponder the mystery of our being. Our conscious minds can grasp only a tiny fraction of the reality in which we are living. How conscious, for example, are any of us of the billions of cells that make up our bodies, each cell as complex in its construction as a galaxy, each cell unique and containing within it the blueprints for the whole body? The cells communicate with one another and provide an ingenious transport system for all the air we breathe and the food and drink we consume. They distribute these elements in such a way that the whole body grows in proportion, so that the bread we eat gives us sight and also enables our toenails to grow. How conscious are we of the extent of these cells' interrelation to every other particle of matter in the universe? Scientists say that when a baby throws its rattle out of the cradle, the planets rock! Our minds, which have the potential to hold all knowledge, are instead liable to be completely preoccupied with the pain of a mild headache or the wound resulting from some- one's criticism! We live, most of the time, totally unaware of how we are interrelated to everything else in creation.

Pondering the mystery of our being helps us to live and see in perspective and gives our minds space to exercise wonder, the beginning of wisdom. When we wonder, we are like that famous painting of Adam in the Sistine chapel: we stretch out our finger to touch the finger of God and catch a glimpse of who we are and what we are called to be.

Religious language is wonder language, opening up our minds to the extraordinary mystery that we are, for "it is in him that we live, and move, and exist" (Acts 17:28). We are images of God. Because God is eternal, always in the now and without past or present, therefore we are.

God is; therefore I am. God cherishes us, considers us precious in his eyes, and so identifies with us that he considers whatever is done to us as also being done to him: "as you did it to one of the least of these who are members of my family, you did it to me" (Matthew 25:40, NRSV). As Christians we believe that the Spirit who lived in Jesus and raised him from the dead lives now in us. We celebrate the Resurrection to remind ourselves that the Spirit of the risen Jesus is with us. God never leaves us, no matter what we may do or not do. "Where could I go to escape your spirit? Where could I flee from your presence? If I climb the heavens, you are there, there too, if I lie in Sheol" (Psalm 139:7–8).

Christ manifests himself differently in each of us. Each of us has a unique role in the life of the universe, to let God be God in our particular circumstances, in our time, in our circle of people. No one can take our place. No higher destiny is possible. What is astonishing is the way in which we manage to distort, discount, and disguise this message and turn our Christian life into something grim, drab, and dreary, which leaves us suspicious of life rather than appreciative of it, guilty and afraid rather than happy and courageous. We can mouth the glorious words that express our faith, but our hearts are not at one with the heart of God's kingdom. They remain firmly lodged in our own kingdom, preserving it, defending it, extending it.

When Jesus began his public life and preaching, his first message was not "Love one another" or even "Love your enemies." It was "The kingdom of God is close at hand. Repent" (Mark 1:15).

The English word *penance* is the translation of the Greek word *metanoia*. The root of *penance* is the Latin word *poena*, which means "punishment," "penalty," "pain," "grief." It is not surprising that Lent, a time for penance, is not our favorite time of the year. *Metanoia*, however, does not mean "punishment" or "pain." Literally, it means "a change of heart." So Lent is not meant to be a time for punishment and pain, but a time for changing our mind, outlook, and attitudes, a time for a change of heart. This point is vividly illustrated in the first reading of Ash Wednesday, when the prophet Joel tells Israel, "Let your hearts be broken, not your garments torn" (Joel 2:13).

As we think, so we are. If we were to believe that every other human being is out to get us, then it would be reasonable for us to walk very carefully along the road, keeping as far away from the pavement as possible lest someone push us into the oncoming traffic. It would also be reasonable for us to look around frequently to see if we are being followed, to inspect every doorway with care lest an assailant be lurking there, and to take special care at road intersections and crossings, where enemy cars can come from four different directions. It would also be reasonable for us to spend a large portion of our income on security gadgets and defense weapons for our homes and perhaps to purchase a grenade or two to carry in our pockets when we do venture outdoors. "For God's sake, stop behaving so stupidly" is a useless exhortation as long as we are still convinced in our minds that every passerby is our enemy. If we are of a religious disposition, we may beseech the Almighty daily with an hour's worth of prayer to protect us from our enemies, and we may fast regularly to give topspin to our prayer. What we need is penance, a change of mind and heart, not to make life harder or to inflict more pain on ourselves but to free ourselves from the intolerable burden that our imaginary fears are imposing on us.

In the Scripture readings in this book, you will find many examples of penance, described as a change of mind and heart that brings freedom, life, joy, and light. "Come to me, all you who labor and are overburdened, and I will give you rest" (Matthew 11:28). "Come now, let us talk this over, says Yahweh. Though your sins are like scarlet, they shall be as white as snow. . . . If you are willing to obey, you shall eat the good things of the earth" (Isaiah 1:18–19). "Pay attention, come to me; listen, and your soul will live" (Isaiah 55:3).

What does a change of mind and heart mean, and how can we make it happen? In a sense, we cannot effect it: all we can do is be attentive to God and let him do the transforming. In a later chapter we will look in more detail at this question of how we can know that a change of mind and heart has taken place and how we can know that it is a turning to God and not a turning in on our own egos.

A real change of mind and heart means an inner surrendering of our own minds and hearts to God so that whatever we do, we do in his Spirit: with him, for him, and through him. We can want to surrender in this way and be sincere in our wanting, but the actual transformation is a lifelong process that is probably completed by few, if any, this side of death. The nearer we approach this surrender, the more we become conscious of the layer upon layer of resistance in our own spirit. That is why so many of the saints, who seem to have lived irreproachable lives, tend to go on and on in their writings about their own sinfulness. It is only those who are near to God who know what sin is. That is why one of the marks of holiness is humility, an unwillingness to condemn or even judge anyone, a great compassion and understanding for the sinner. Such attitudes are called "soft" by hard-liners who, having no knowledge of their own sinfulness, see it clearly in everyone else. Beware of religious men and women who know all about God and his ways, especially in his intentions for others, and lack gentleness! Rabbi Lionel Blue, in the radio program *Thought for the Day*, once described the genuinely religious person as one who cares for his or her own soul but for everyone else's body, while the hypocrite cares for everyone else's soul and for his or her own body.

God is constantly nudging us toward a change of mind and heart. Our difficulty is in recognizing his nudging. Deep within us, no matter how irreligious, unspiritual, or unprayerful we may feel or think we are, is an innate longing for God, the longing Augustine recognized as he looked back on his life and wrote, "Lord, you created me for yourself, and my heart is restless until it rests in you." In our consciousness, this drawing to God may feel ungodly; we may experience feelings of boredom, dissatisfaction, disappointment, disgust, emptiness, darkness, isolation, and estrangement even from those closest to us. God is in all things, even in our negative feelings, and if we can allow these feelings to come into our prayer, we can begin to see them as God's invitation to us to change. The impression given in some Christian circles is that those who are close to God live in a constant state of bliss, full of the love of God and his creation, safely cocooned from any negative emotions. This is not the experience of the saints. Those who preach that people who have turned to God no longer experience darkness or any negative emotions can never have met God in their own prayer and cannot know themselves, but they can prevent others from finding him. That is why it is so important for us, as we will see later in this book, to bring all our moods and feelings into prayer so that we can recognize God's nudgings in all of our experience.

Who is this God whom we are called to allow inside us? Only God can teach us who God is, and he teaches each of us in a different way through the circumstances of our own lives. We have no other way of knowing him. We can learn about him from books, from teachers, and from other people, but we can know him only with our own hearts. That is why prayer has been described as "heart speaking to heart," a better description of prayer than the more common "raising the mind and heart to God." In prayer we do try to raise our minds and hearts to God, but the very word "raise" can mislead us into thinking that God is only above and beyond us and not also within us, more present to us than we are to ourselves. When we concentrate on God above, we tend to think of him as apart from our daily concerns, and this is one of the fundamental difficulties most of us experience when we try to pray. We try to raise our minds and hearts to God beyond us and try to banish what we call "distractions," as though God cannot be interested or present in our preoccupations. We find nothing in the beyond and soon find our minds filled with a torrent of thoughts, imaginings, and emotions that are all very earthy and seem to have nothing to do with God above and may even seem opposed to him.

The circumstances of our lives are not "distractions." The word *distraction* is based on a Latin root that means to "draw apart" or "drag away." The facts of our lives are not distractions; they do not drag us away from God but are the place, and the only place, where we can meet God, for that is where he is for us. When we ignore the facts of our existence in prayer, all that we meet is an abstraction. Therefore, to try to raise our minds and hearts to God as though he were not present in the facts of our lives is a distraction, and to pray to God while attending to what is going on within and around us is an attraction to God. It is only by reflecting on the circumstances of our own lives and on the reality around us that we can begin to know God and then come to know that he is also beyond us. Just as the first disciples came to a knowledge of Jesus as Christ, Son of the living God, only through first knowing him as a human being, so can we come to know God within and around us only through our own human experience. The early church writers spoke of creation itself as a sacrament of God; that is, as a sign— an effective sign—of his presence.

Therefore, nothing in creation, no experience of life, is necessarily a distraction. Everything that happens to us is an invitation from God to turn to him. Prayer is as wide as creation: every experience can become a prayer. It is because we have forgotten this fundamental truth that our Christian spirituality so often seems artificial, out of touch, contrived. We think of it as the private property of a few, a treasured possession. It can encase us in unshakable self-righteousness, concerned with everyone else's spiritual welfare and our own material security.

God is both beyond us and within us. Theologians speak of God as transcendent and immanent. By "transcendent" they mean that God is always greater, too great for our finite minds to adequately grasp, define, or contain. For us, God will always be mystery; the more we come to know him, the more there is to know. "My ways are above your ways, my thoughts above your thoughts," says the Lord God (Isaiah 55:9). Our temptation is always to cut God down to our size, to make him in our own image, to control and domesticate him so that he always acts predictably and is always on our side. In war memorials, the dead of both sides gave their lives *pro Deo et patria*, "for God and country." But God cannot be controlled in this way. He cannot be held within any human definition. He is always greater, unpredictable. This truth is often very disturbing and painful for us. When afflicted with tragedy, we ask, "How could God allow this to happen to me?"

The church is the sacrament of God in the world, an effective sign of his presence with us. Consequently, the church must reflect this transcendent quality of God, this characteristic unpredictability, this surprise element, by being a developing church or, as the early church described itself, "a pilgrim church," always on the move, on a journey out of the slavery of Egypt, through the wilderness, and into the Promised Land. This truth about the church can also be very painful and disturbing to us and is the root cause of much of the bitterness, animosity, and divisiveness between and within Christian churches. Even the slightest change can cause a major disturbance within church congregations, and nothing is more divisive in most congregations than a change in divine service. We all fear change and long for security, but a church that offers us nothing but stability has ceased to be a part of the church and is no longer a sign of the transcendent God.

God is also immanent, present in all things, but contained by none: "it is in him that we live, and move, and exist" (Acts 17:28). The Bible is the story of the immanence of the transcendent God in the history of Israel, a history which, like our own, is often messy and problematic. Yet this obscure and troubled Middle East nation was destined by God to be a light to all nations.

> At various times in the past and in various different ways, God spoke to our ancestors through the prophets; but in our own time, the last days, he has spoken to us through his Son, the Son that he has appointed to inherit everything and through whom he made everything there is. He is the radiant light of God's glory and the perfect copy of his nature, sustaining the universe by his powerful command.
>
> Hebrews 1:1–3

The transcendent God, expressed in Jesus, is a light that shines in the darkness. Because the darkness could not understand the light, it tried to destroy it. "It is better for one man to die for the people," said Caiaphas (John 18:14). But the darkness could not overpower the light, for God, in Jesus, entered into our death and became sin for us (2 Corinthians 5:21) and is risen from the dead. The Spirit that lived in Jesus and raised him from the dead now lives in us. How do we recognize his Spirit within us? We have looked at God's transcendence and his immanence, but that still has not answered the question What is God like? John gives the astounding answer "God is love." In a school where I once taught, an infuriated teacher of religion ordered a class to write out a hundred times "God is love." We can hear this phrase, or even write it out a thousand times, but it bounces off the top layer of our minds without effecting any change of heart. Penitence is about letting these phrases sink into those levels of consciousness where change occurs. And that is the subject of the next chapter.

Chapter 3

Some Ways of Praying

THERE ARE AS MANY DIFFERENT WAYS OF PRAYING AS THERE are human beings. Prayer is about being ourselves before God. He creates each one of us as unique, distinguishable from every other human being, for example, by our finger-prints, voiceprints, cell prints, handwriting, and manner-isms, so it is not surprising that we should each pray in a different way. Yet we often forget this obvious truth, especially when we read books on prayer that give the impression that praying is like operating a washing machine: if you follow the instructions, you will get the desired results. If you do not follow the instructions, then something is wrong with you, so go back and read the directions or call in an expert.

This chapter does not contain the last word on ways of praying, but it does offer some suggestions on how to find one's own unique way of praying that many people have found helpful. I have met so many people who say, "I can't pray," or "I find praying boring and do not know what I am supposed to be doing," or "I recite prayers, read the Scripture, and feel as though nothing is happening. It gets me nowhere." Yet so many of these same people, once they have been encouraged to experiment with new ways of praying, find prayer absorbing, fascinating in itself and in the effect it has on their lives. But before you read further, it is also only fair for me to say that they also wish, at times, that they had never started praying, because God can sometimes be very uncomfortable to live with while at other times he seems to be profoundly deaf!

One of the major obstacles to prayer is our image of God. We can come to know God only through our human experience. It is easy to say, "God is love," but my experience of love may have been traumatic, an experience of pain, betrayal, and rejection. It is questionable whether any human being is capable of unconditional love. Even the most perfect parents and teachers tend to place conditions on their love, and some do so very explicitly. We learn at a very early age that love is to be earned: like everything else, it is subject to market forces!

When I was a university chaplain in the late sixties and early seventies, I spent much of my time talking with students who had either rejected their faith or were thinking about doing so. After many conversations with these students, a profile of God formed in my imagination. God became "good old Uncle George," the favorite of the family, wealthy, powerful, influential, wise, and loving to us all. As children, we are taken to visit him, an old man with a deep voice, in his mansion. At the end of the visit he turns to us and says, "I want to see you here, dear, every Sunday, and I'll now show you what will happen if you don't come." He leads us to the basement, which is very dark and hot, and we hear bloodcurdling screams. We see rows of steel doors. Uncle George opens one to reveal a huge room full of furnaces into which long rows of men, women, and children are being hurled by little demons. "And that, my dear, is what will happen to you if you don't visit me regularly." We are delivered back, shaking with terror, to our loving parents. Clutching both of them we proceed home. Mother bends down to us and says, "Now don't you love Uncle George with all your heart and soul and strength?" And we, remembering the furnaces, answer, "Yes, I do." In our hearts we loathe him as a monster, but our hearts will put us in the furnace, so we agree with Mother.

This is a caricature, but it illustrates the truth that we have inherited unique and very deformed images of God. When we are children, God may be Uncle George for one child and a vague Santa Claus figure—to be called on at Christmas, Easter, baptisms, weddings, and funerals, but safely ignored the rest of the time—for another. And although we may recognize the deformity of our image of God as we grow up, a felt knowledge remains deep in our subconscious minds and affects our mental and emotional states, leaving us addicted to anxiety-ridden religious observance or with a deep distaste for anything religious. Our religious vocabulary often reflects the deformity. We talk of Lent, for example, as a time for penance, for turning back to God, and so associate God with the states of pain, punishment, suffering, penalty, and grief to which the origins of the word refer. Yet the New Testament word for "penance," as we have seen, is *metanoia*, a change of mind and heart, a turning back to a God who is described as our freedom and our delight, the one for whom our soul longs, the joy of our desiring.

We may know intellectually that God is not cruel, sadistic, or capricious or that he is not Santa Claus, but when we try to pray, that is the kind of God we may meet, for our childhood impressions are not easily eradicated. God can be known by God alone, and God tells us through the psalmist, "Be still, and know that I am God!" (Psalm 46:10, NRSV), so if we are to recognize God in our lives, we must learn to be still.

It is difficult enough for most of us to be physically still for any length of time, but it is even more difficult to be mentally still. Fortunately, our minds are so constructed that we can concentrate on only one thing at a time. If I concentrate my whole attention on what I am feeling in my big toe, I cannot be thinking about God or anything else at the same time. Here is an exercise in being still:

Sit on a chair or on the floor in as relaxed a way as you can, keeping your back straight without being rigid. Now focus your attention on what you can feel in your body. You might start with your right foot, then travel slowly around your body, not thinking about what you are feeling, but just feeling. This exercise could not be simpler, yet most of us find it very difficult, for no sooner have we begun than our thinking mind distracts us, asking us if we are not wasting our time, reminding us of the things we have to do and of the things we have left undone, wondering what this exercise has to do with prayer in general, and with our own spiritual journey in particular. As soon as you become conscious of the mind's activity, acknowledge the thoughts and questions as interesting, but bring your attention back to what you are feeling. Similarly, if you feel uncomfortable, acknowledge the discomfort, but return your attention to what you are feeling in your body. The longer you can spend concentrating on one part of your body, the better. Experts in this art of being still can sit motionless for an hour or more, concentrating their whole attention, for example, on their upper lip. There is no need for you to be this ambitious; even a few minutes can be helpful.

Once you feel relaxed in this exercise, you may want to make it more explicitly a prayer, using that phrase that Paul used: "it is in him that we live, and move, and exist" (Acts 17:28). Where is God? God is where we are. He is our life and our consciousness, nearer to us than we are to ourselves. This truth, that God is where we are, is the basis of all the prayer methods described in this chapter.

In doing this exercise, it is interesting to note how our thinking mind will not allow us to concentrate on the immediate present but is constantly drawing us into the future or the past. Because this habit allows us to give only a fraction of our attention to the immediate present, the only reality we have at the moment, it is destructive. By concentrating on the past and the future, we spend most of our time escaping from reality. A good spiritual exercise would be to try to live as fully as possible in the present moment.

God is where we are, and there is no other place where we can find him. This is another obvious truth that we so often forget in practice. We put God "out there," or in the church, or in some other holy place. Because we externalize God and live in the past or in the future, we can waste our lives in fruitless regrets about what we might have been, or could become, if only our circumstances were different.

What is God's will for you now? It is to be found precisely where you are at the moment, in this place, with your family, in your community, in your work, with this temperament and these gifts, abilities, disabilities, and sinful tendencies. It is from this point and from no other that you are to find him, and it is from these circumstances and from no others that you will be glorified. This does not mean that we have to stay where we are and as we are. Our feelings of discontent are his nudgings, encouraging us to change either our situation or the way in which we perceive it. The only way we can find him is by starting from where we are; otherwise, we are like the person who, on being asked directions to a village, began with, "If I were you, I wouldn't start from here."

Another stillness exercise involves sitting as you did for the previous exercise but concentrating this time on your breathing, the physical feeling of breathing in and breathing out. Breathe naturally; you may find that your breathing deepens. Some people find that when they pay attention to their breathing, their breath quickens. If this persists and causes breathlessness, abandon the exercise. When you feel still, this exercise too may be turned into a prayer. Let the breathing in express all that you long for. Scripture describes God as the breath, the Spirit, the giver of life. You are meeting him in your breathing, so let his life flow into you, into every part of your body and into the recesses of your mind and heart. Let God be God to you. Let the breathing out express your longing to hand yourself and all your worries, anxieties, fears, and guilty feelings over to him. Don't judge yourself; just hurl yourself at him.

It is good to begin each prayer period with one of these stillness exercises. If you find them helpful and do not want to do anything else in the time you have set aside for your prayer, then continue with them. This is another useful guideline for prayer: we should always follow our instincts and pray as we can, not as we can't. Most of us can easily agree with this advice and readily give it to others, but we find it very difficult to follow it ourselves. This is because we have been assured from an early age that others know best, that we must follow the rules that the more learned or experienced lay down for us. While it is important to take note of the learned and the wise, it is also important to listen to our own wisdom, for if we ignore or discount it we may also be ignoring the promptings of God, who is dwelling within us. We should listen to our own wisdom not only in deciding what to pray but also in how to pray, whether we should kneel, sit, stand, lie down, or walk, and for how long.

All the Scripture readings I have chosen for this book are intended to help us turn back to God or, as the Gospel translation puts it, to repent of our sins. Evagrius, an ancient theologian, said, "Sin is forgetfulness of God's goodness." All sin is an offense against goodness and love, and love alone can overcome sin. We cannot overcome sin by berating or punishing ourselves because self-disapproval usually locks us more securely in our own destructiveness. The first step toward repentance is to turn our attention to God's goodness. God alone can teach us what sin is.

How can we focus our attention on the goodness of God? God, and still more, his goodness, can seem to us to be very abstract concepts, especially when we are the victims of other people's meanness or cruelty or feel caught in our own.

Before we go to sleep, we tend to recall the events of the day, especially if we have had a disagreement with someone. We replay the incident, adjusting it to our advantage and kicking ourselves for having been so slow-witted at the time, for now we have thought of the cutting remark that would have demolished the opposition. Instead of recalling the bad moments of the day, we can use this natural tendency to recall the good moments, the moments we enjoyed; we should relish and appreciate them no matter how trivial they may seem. What surprises most people when they first do this exercise is how many enjoyable incidents they discover in that day for which they are grateful. It is only by looking at, appreciating, and relishing such moments in our lives that we can come to any real notion of God's goodness. We must see these moments as God's gifts to us, not because we have been good or have worked hard, have been virtuous or loyal, but because we are precious in God's eyes and he loves us (Isaiah 43:4). Doing this exercise once may have little aftereffect, but if it becomes habitual it will begin to change our perception, the basis of all change. We will begin to see our present reality not simply as an impersonal set of circumstances set up to try us, a kind of divine obstacle course with eternal penalties awaiting the losers, but as a life filled with the presence of a beckoning and loving God, a God who delights in giving, a God who is much more for us than we can possibly be for ourselves. When we can begin to perceive our reality in this way, it will be as though everything has been transformed, as though we have moved from an impersonal institution to home, where everything speaks of those we love. The change is well expressed in Joseph Plunkett's poem "I See His Blood upon the Rose":

I see His blood upon the rose
And in the stars the glory of His eyes,
His body gleams amid eternal snows,
His tears fall from the skies.
I see His face in every flower;
The thunder and the singing of the birds
Are but His voice—and carven by His power
Rocks are His written words.
All pathways by His feet are worn,
His strong heart stirs the ever-beating sea,
His crown of thorns is twined with every thorn,
His cross is every tree.

It is only by thanking God for his gifts that we can come to know him, the giver, and it is only by knowing his goodness that we can begin to know what repentance means. So thank him each evening for the people and events you have enjoyed each day.

Before you pray, it is good to stand a step away from your prayer place for a moment and think about what it is that you are about to do. Then, in whatever posture enables you to be both relaxed and attentive, beg God that everything within you may be directed to his praise and service.

As Christians, we pray from the Scriptures in the belief that these books, although written by very different people at different times and in very different styles, are God's communication to us now. We read them not primarily to learn what God was doing with Israel two or three thousand years ago but to understand, through the medium of these readings, what God is doing with us now. In a sense, the Bible is of secondary importance; what is of primary importance is the present, what God is doing now. In the light of the Scripture texts we can begin to recognize God in our "now."

People pray from Scripture in many different ways. In monasteries, before there were printed texts, the monks would gather and one of them would read aloud a passage from a manuscript. He would choose a short passage, read it slowly, and keep repeating it. As he read, the monks would get up and leave to return to their private cells. They were leaving not because they were bored but because they had found a word or phrase in the readings that they liked and on which they could pray. They would then focus their attention on this word or phrase, hear it speak to them, relish and savor it, and tell God from their hearts what thoughts and feelings the word had evoked.

To illustrate this method, let us consider 2 Corinthians 5:20–6:2, "We are ambassadors for Christ; it is as though God were appealing through us, and the appeal that we make in Christ's name is: be reconciled to God. For our sake God made the sinless one into sin, so that in him we might become the goodness of God. As his fellow workers, we beg you once again not to neglect the grace of God that you have received. For he says: 'At the favorable time, I have listened to you; on the day of salvation I came to your help.' Well, now is the favorable time; this is the day of salvation."

Read the passage several times. Make no attempt to analyze it, but notice whether any word or phrase stands out for you. Suppose the phrase is "For our sake God made the sinless one into sin, so that in him we might become the goodness of God." Keep hearing it spoken to you, as though God is now saying, "It was for your sake . . . so that you might become the goodness of God." How do you react to this? With disbelief? amazement? bewilderment? doubt? delight? anxiety? There is no right or wrong response; whatever response you feel, whatever thoughts or reflections arise from the passage, present them to God and talk to him about them. Your prayer cannot be too simple, too direct, too childlike.

Each person prays differently, but most of us find that although we may start well, after a minute or two our minds begin to fragment into thoughts and images that have nothing to do with becoming the goodness of God. We may be deep into feelings of resentment toward someone, or worrying about our health or money problems, or thinking about the latest TV program. Such wanderings of attention are sometimes called "distractions," and we are often told that we should banish them from our minds. The trouble with distractions is that the more we try to get rid of them, the more they pester us. Instead, let the distractions come into your prayer. Remember, anything can be used in prayer.

In this method of prayer, the word or phrase that catches our attention may be compared to a searchlight. We focus on it for a while but soon become aware of a flow of consciousness in us. This stream of thoughts, feelings, and desires seems at first to be a distraction. But it can become the very substance of our prayer if we let the phrase or word play on it like a light before we pray to God out of it. For example, the phrase "You are to become the goodness of God" may have caught my attention, yet I find myself sunk in a mood of resentment toward someone. By letting the phrase "You are to become the goodness of God" hover over my feelings of resentment, I may begin to feel uncomfortable and want either to stop hearing the phrase or stop thinking about my resentment. Instead, I have to try to hold the two of them together. This may be uncomfortable, for I may find that my resentment is much more powerful and attractive to me than any hope of becoming the goodness of God. Before my "distraction" appeared, I felt moved by this phrase, but once I apply the phrase to my distraction, I begin to realize the strength of my resentment and the unreal nature of my attraction to God, which is strong enough in my holy moments or when I am singing a hymn but quite useless in everyday life. This is an unpleasant discovery for me to make and may feel like a spiritual failure, but in fact the prayer is working very well for me. The word of God is a double-edged sword: we feel uncomfortable by what it reveals to us while at the same time it is penetrating the top layer of our consciousness to the deeper layers below, revealing what is there. We may not like what we see; we may be horrified to discover that we are not the objective, fair, and noble-minded person we thought we were but that we dwell in and act out of dark areas of meanness, love-lessness, and distrust within us. In prayer it is important to let these areas come to the surface and expose them to the word of God. This is the spiritual struggle, the unmasking of the demons. We experience our own helplessness and are forced to pray out of our need. We begin to see that the behavior of the person who has caused us such feelings of resentment is our problem too. The splinter in our brother's eye has become the beam in our own, but if we can acknowledge it and show it to God, we will find him to be the God of mercy and compassion, much gentler toward us than we can ever be to ourselves.

Any passage of Scripture can be prayed imaginatively, but Gospel passages are especially suitable for this next kind of prayer. Imagine that the scene in the reading is happening as you pray. You are not simply observing it; you are an active participant in the scene, so you can talk to Jesus and the other characters in the scene.

As in the previous method of prayer, begin by pausing for a moment by the place where you are going to pray and begging God that everything within you may be directed to his praise and service. Read the passage several times until it is familiar to you, then put it aside and try to imagine the scene. I'll use the following short passage to illustrate the method:

> In the evening of that same day, the first day of the week, the doors were closed in the room where the disciples were, for fear of the Jews. Jesus came and stood among them. He said to them, "Peace be with you," and showed them his hands and his side. The disciples were filled with joy when they saw the Lord, and he said to them again, "Peace be with you. As the Father sent me, so am I sending you."
>
> JOHN 20:19–21

Imagine yourself walking up the stairs outside the house to an upper room. It does not matter if you have no idea what Jerusalem looks like now or two thousand years ago. See what picture presents itself, however vaguely. The door is opened to you and you enter a room. What kind of room do you see? Don't be in a hurry—let the picture come to you gradually. Can you see people in the room? What are they doing? What are they saying, or are they in silence? What is the mood of the room? You might want to talk to some of the people present. They are afraid. You can share with them your own fears, whatever they are. Take your time in doing this. "Jesus came and stood among them." Can you see the sudden change in the disciples? Can you hear Jesus say to you, "Peace be with you" and see him showing you his hands and side? Listen, watch, be silent, or speak; do whatever you feel prompted to do. Be simple, childlike, and spontaneous and let your imagination take you where it will, as long as it is helping you to pray. If you catch your attention straying from the scene or your mind leading you apart from it with speculative questions like "How do we know what really happened?" and "Is there really a physical resurrection?" acknowledge these as interesting questions, but bring yourself back into the scene. What you are doing is encountering the risen Lord, present within you, through the medium of your imagination. When you talk with him in your imagination, the scene may disappear altogether and you may find yourself talking to him now, which is where he is for you.

Many people, on being first introduced to this way of praying, may reject it before trying it, saying, "But I have no imagination." Everyone has an imagination of some kind, so give it a try. Your imagination may not be very visual, and so you may not see details with any clarity, but you can say to yourself, "Peace be with you," knowing it is Christ speaking to you now, and you can respond, perhaps with thanks or with disbelief, irritation, or anger. Whatever happens within you, show it to Christ and talk with him about it. In this way you are letting his presence and his peace enter into the deeper layers of your mind and heart where change occurs.

Our imagination does not present truth, but it reflects aspects of ourselves of which we often were previously unaware. This is an important point to understand because otherwise, we can misinterpret what imagination reveals. For example, one person praying this passage found that Jesus, instead of turning to her to say, "Peace be with you," turned away from her, which caused her great distress. What her imagination was showing was not Christ's rejection of her but an aspect of herself. Because she had experienced rejection by her parents in the past, she found it hard to believe that there was anyone who would not reject her, God included. This example shows why it is important to return to those moments in prayer when we have experienced feelings of rejection or isolation and pray with the psalmist, "Lord, show me your face."

Prayer is not always a beautiful experience. It can also be a very stormy one, but this is a sign that we really are engaging with God. In the next chapter we will look at these variations in mood, what they mean and how to cope with them.

When you finish praying, it is good to spend a few minutes reflecting on what happened, noting what you felt and what caused those feelings. Did you experience feelings of peace or agitation, happiness or sadness, hope or hopelessness, love or hate, interest or boredom? Let us suppose that I have felt thoroughly bored and distracted throughout the prayer period. I notice this in the reflection and then ask myself what caused the boredom. I look more closely at the prayer and realize that once it began, I hardly gave God a thought, while my mind was hopping over my many preoccupations and worries. Whose kingdom has preoccupied me, Christ's or my own? I realize it was my own and that I never even referred my preoccupations to Christ. The prayer period has not been a failure, provided that the next time I pray I try to refer all my preoccupations to God.

If I have experienced moments of peace, happiness, hope, and strength during the prayer, I should then note what gave rise to those feelings, whether a phrase or word of Scripture, an image, or a memory. In my next prayer period I should go back to that phrase or word and stay with it for as long as I can. This habit of reflecting on our last prayer in our next prayer period, returning to its good moments first and then returning to its less good moments, is a way of inviting God to enter the deeper layers of our consciousness.

In the next chapter we shall look at these variations in mood and feeling more closely to understand their meaning and how to cope with them.

Chapter 4

Finding Direction through Prayer

AS I AM WRITING, A FIERCE WIND IS BLOWING THROUGH THE closed, single-glazed window. Outside, the sky is dappled with shades of gray and short-lived patches of blue. It is a welcome sight after the monochrome gray of January and February.

The sky reflects our inner landscape, the moods and feelings that arise in our consciousness, affecting our perception of and reaction to life around us. Along our inner journey we experience darkness and light, blizzards and sunshine, hail and rain, gales and calm. What do these inner states mean, and how are we to react to them? If on a walking pilgrimage I am willing to walk only when the temperature is above sixty degrees and below eighty, the wind at my back and the sun shining, then I am not likely to make much progress toward my destination on most days of the year.

This also applies to our inner journey: if we can operate only when feeling well and full of enthusiasm, many of us will be doomed to lives of inactivity. Prayer puts us in touch with our inner landscape, but if we pray only when the weather is favorable, that is, when we feel good about it and experience peace, assurance, happiness, and confidence, then we will learn little about our inner journey and will remain imprisoned behind the bars of our unquestioning minds.

These inner moods and feelings are direction signs for us. To ignore them is like setting out on a journey to an unknown destination without maps or a compass. Who would be so foolish? Yet this folly is considered wisdom by those who teach us to ignore our feelings both in prayer and out of it. On a journey it is counterproductive to follow every signpost, but it is still more useless to ignore them all. Wisdom lies in deciding which signs to follow.

A good example of the significance of feelings can be found in the conversion story of Iñigo of Loyola, a Basque nobleman of fiery temperament and uncertain morals who later founded the Jesuit Order and is now known as St. Ignatius of Loyola. In his late twenties, Iñigo suffered bad leg injuries when he was struck with a cannonball. He whiled away his convalescence daydreaming of the heroic deeds he would do upon recovery and of the great lady he would win. He had such a gift for daydreaming that he could lose himself in a reverie for three hours at a time. Then he would grow bored and ask for novels. But because Loyola Castle, where he lived, did not have any novels, he had to make do with the only books they could supply, books on the life of Christ and the lives of the saints. He began daydreaming about becoming a great saint, out-stripping the lot of them with his austerities and goodness. For weeks he alternated between the two sets of daydreams, and then he noticed something that would change his life.

Both sets of daydreams were pleasant at the time, but the aftereffects were different. Heroic deeds and the great lady left him bored, empty, and sad; outdoing the saints left him happy, strengthened, and hopeful. He later called this experience his first lesson in "discerning the spirits," which we might call reading our inner moods.

Saying, "Do your duty and ignore your feelings" is like saying to the motorist, "Ignore the state of your engine and just follow the highway code," advice that, if followed, would soon cause the roadways to clog with broken-down cars. *Emotion* is an interesting word. Literally, it means "that which causes movement." Without emotions we stop living: if we ignore or repress them, we crash.

Our emotions are very complex, and they are more numerous than the instruments in a large orchestra. Usually many are playing in us at the same time, producing agony, ecstasy, or just indeterminate noise.

One evening I watched an episode of "One Man and His Dog," a television series that documents sheepdog trials, and found the program to be an excellent portrayal of our inner life. The sheep correspond to our various emotions, appetites, desires, ideals, fears, hopes, and ambitions, while the sheepdog corresponds to the deepest part of ourselves, sometimes called "the fine point of the soul," our truest self, that which in our wildest dreams we would love to become. Iñigo, in his daydreams about outdoing the saints, was getting in touch with the sheepdog part of himself.

The sheepdog may be intelligent, fast, and strong, but unless it has a good relationship with the shepherd, it will fail to bring the sheep through the gate and will probably damage them. What corresponds to the sheepdog/shepherd relationship in us?

Augustine, looking back on his life, concluded, "Lord, you created me for yourself, and my heart is restless until it rests in you." We come from God, our origin, and return to him, our destination. Like Augustine, for most of our lives we are not aware that this is our nature. What we are conscious of is the bleating of our sheep, the cries of our inner desires for satisfaction. We try to answer them and are thwarted, or we succeed and are disappointed, hurting ourselves and others in the process. "The fine point of the soul" seems to be just an empty phrase, a phrase that is nonexistent in us or buried beneath the debris of broken dreams and shattered hopes.

Iñigo decided to start outdoing the saints by going on a pilgrimage to Jerusalem, such a risky undertaking in the sixteenth century that pilgrims were advised to make a general confession before starting out. Iñigo had so much to confess that it took him three days. He then spent nine months in a cave at Manresa, where he underwent spiritual experiences of darkness and light. Out of this experience he eventually wrote his Spiritual Exercises, a series of Scripture-based meditations and contemplations designed to bring the creative and destructive movements within us to consciousness so that we can follow the creative, get rid of the destructive, and in the process find the will of God for us. When he finished the Exercises he added a short preface, a skeletal summary of the contents that was itself summarized in his opening sentence, "Man is created to praise, reverence, and serve God our Lord, and by this means to save his soul" (translation mine). This is a traditional Christian statement of the purpose of human life. Other well-known formulations are "We are created to know, love, and serve

God," or Paul's "Before the world was made, he chose us, chose us in Christ . . . to live through love in his presence" (Ephesians 1:4).

All these formulations may be compared to oil drills. We have to let them sink into our minds and hearts until they reach the fine point of the soul, where we can recognize them not as precepts imposed on us from without but as the voice of our own soul expressing its deepest longing. Then we can, like Augustine, begin to recognize the true meaning of much of our pain, disappointment, emptiness, disillusionment, and restlessness. The fine point of the soul is of God, and it can find no rest except in him. When the fine point of the soul, the core of our being, is directed toward God, then all our attitudes, values, decisions, and actions that are in accord with that fundamental direction will resonate in us. They will bring peace, tranquillity, and strength while the destructive elements within us and outside us will jar us, causing agitation, sadness, and inner turmoil.

What does it mean to be directed toward God? As we have already seen, we can have all kinds of deformed and destructive images of God, which explains why so many crimes have been committed in the name of God. We can come to knowledge of God only in and through his creation; we have no other option. When Ignatius says, "We are created to praise, reverence, and serve God," what does he mean? The phrase can suggest a God with a voracious appetite for adulation matched only by his delight in the destruction of those who do not comply with his appetite.

In our human experience, praise is genuine only if it is based on appreciation of someone or something. We can know God only through his creation. Therefore we can praise him only insofar as we can appreciate, value, cherish, love, and enjoy his creation. The psalms are full of praise, but it is praise of God's creation. One Jewish writer has said that the first and only question God will put to us at the Final Judgment will be, "Did you enjoy my creation?" That is why recalling each day and thanking God for the things we have enjoyed is so important. God does not need our praise, but we need to praise him so that we can begin to recognize his beckoning presence in everyday life.

The way we relate to God's creation, especially the way we relate to one another, is the way we relate to him. "In so far as you did this to one of the least of these brothers [or sisters] of mine, you did it to me" (Matthew 25:40). "Love your enemies and pray for those who persecute you; in this way you will be sons of your Father in heaven, for he causes his sun to rise on bad men as well as good, and his rain to fall on honest and dishonest men alike. . . . You must therefore be perfect just as your heavenly Father is perfect" (Matthew 5:44–45, 48).

To be turned toward God in the core of our being is, as the prophet Micah puts it, "to act justly, to love tenderly and to walk humbly with your God" (Micah 6:8). The fine point of the soul wants to do this, but when we try to put it into practice, we discover inner opposition. For example, acting justly may result in a decrease in my income, but my love of wealth is like a recalcitrant sheep that refuses to obey the sheepdog, so I ignore the fine point of my soul and pursue my own immediate gain. Or acting justly may make me unpopular with my colleagues or perhaps put my job at risk, so I decide to ignore the cause of justice and truth in favor of my popularity, position, and security. My love of wealth, status, self-importance, health, and fame corresponds to the sheep in me that are often in opposition to the sheepdog, the fine point of the soul, and this conflict registers in my feelings and emotions.

All our inner moods and feelings arise out of our desires. When our desires are satisfied, we are content; when they are thwarted, we feel frustrated. Whatever we experience within ourselves, it is good to ask ourselves the question "What is the underlying desire? Is it a desire to 'praise, reverence, and serve God,' or is it a desire to be praised, reverenced, and served?" Another way of questioning our inner feelings is to ask, "Whose kingdom is being affected, mine or God's?" In this way we can begin to see more clearly what is creative in us and what is destructive.

Here is a version of St. Ignatius's preface to his *Spiritual Exercises*. It is not a translation, but I hope the more contemporary language better conveys the meaning of the sixteenth-century text.

> Before the world was made, we were chosen to live lovingly in God's presence by praising, reverencing, and serving him in and through his creation. As God is in all things and in all circumstances, we must appreciate and make use of everything that draws us to God, and rid ourselves of whatever prevents us from living before him in love. Therefore we must be so poised [detached/indifferent] that we do not cling to any created thing as though it were our ultimate good, but remain open to the possibility that love may demand of us poverty rather than riches, sickness rather than health, dishonor rather than honor, a short life rather than a long one, because God alone is our security, our refuge, and our strength. We can be so detached from any created

thing only if we have a stronger attachment; therefore our one dominating desire and fundamental
choice must be to live in love in his presence.

When we get in touch with this dominating desire and
fundamental choice, the sheepdog part of us begins to move
and encounter the reluctant sheep—our unwillingness to
change, our love of our own security, and so on—and it
inspires fear, anxiety, and even panic in us. In the rest of
this chapter I will give a few guidelines to help readers to
react to and interpret for themselves the feelings they
experience in prayer and out of it. The guidelines will help
only to some extent because our inner moods and feelings
are very complex and it is only gradually and with practice
that we come to know them and learn to distinguish the
creative from the destructive.

These guidelines are a shortened and simplified version
of "The Rules for Discernment of Spirits" that Ignatius
gives in *The Spiritual Exercises.* Read these guidelines slowly
and see if they correspond to your own experience, for
they will be of use to you only insofar as they do. Do not
worry if you feel you have not completely understood them
the first time. As you go through the guidelines, try to
relate them to your own experience and see whether they
are true for you. You may like to make up your own
guidelines, which can help you to understand better what
is going on in your own prayer and make you a better
listener to other people's prayer experience if you meet
in a sharing group.

1. *Direct the core of your being toward God.*

When you do this, the decisions you make, which are in

harmony with that fundamental choice, will resonate in your moods and feelings, bringing with them some measure of peace, strength, and tranquillity. The destructive forces outside and within us will oppose this fundamental desire, causing agitation, sadness, and inner turmoil.

A friend of mine named Father Michael Ivens was quite involved in the charismatic movement when it first reached Britain in the early seventies. He divided the charismatics into two classes, the airborne and the crashed, and said that the crashed were by far the most difficult to work with. The charismatics have come a long way since then, but in the early days the crashed were those who believed that once they had turned to Jesus and had been born again, the delight, joy, and freedom they experienced should last till death. When it did not, they began to doubt their initial experience of joy and delight, to feel that they no longer had faith or that there was no God in whom they could believe. They did not realize that those who have turned to God are not exempt from states of agitation, sadness, and doubt.

A few years ago, I was walking along the vale of Clwyd, a river in north Wales, when I spotted the ruins of a church in a meadow. It was a small fifteenth-century church, its stone walls still standing. Outside the north wall was a well of springwater enclosed in carved stone shaped like the center of a Celtic cross. An underground stream fed the well with such force that the wellspring was visible at its center. It was a bright autumn day, so clear that I could see tiny motes dancing to the flow of water in the center of the well. The edges of the well were covered in dead leaves and the water was muddy. This picture has stayed in my memory because for me it was another image of life.

One of the tiny motes dancing in the wellspring represents our human consciousness, which can make universal statements like "The universe began with a big bang thirteen billion years ago," or "The universe did not begin in this way," but can, in fact, grasp very little. To say that our human knowledge is equal to one thirteen-billionth of our ignorance is exaggerating the extent of our knowledge.

The Eucharistic preface in the Roman Missal begins "It is right and fitting, our duty, and it leads to our salvation that we should thank you always and everywhere," but it is also right and fitting that we should ponder frequently our own ignorance. Because we do not, we are given to making universal statements about life, statements that are based on our own profound ignorance and arrogance, uttering them with certainty and often imposing them on others.

I thought of the little mote dancing in the water and imagined it saying to itself, "I have been baptized in the Spirit, washed white in the blood of the Lamb; I am safe in God's hands; he loves and protects me, supports and enlivens me. God is good and life is wonderful. Praise the Lord." Then, through the movement of water and wind, the little mote moves off center and ends up among the dead leaves and mud at the well's edge. It is now saying, "I am lost and in darkness and this is the truth of things. There is no way out. I am trapped. I can't trust anyone or anything, least of all my own experience. Religion is the opiate of the people. The reality is this chaos and darkness." Our consciousness is depicted as the mote, and both sets of statements come out of our own ignorance and arrogance.

Yes, as a human being I am in God's hands. As each cell of the body contains every other, so each human being contains every other, affects every other, and is affected by each. As we move closer to God, we become more aware of the unity and interdependence of all things. We come to understand that our true self is all embracing, that our ego self is largely illusion, and that we are all immersed in the well of life, the well of light and darkness, clarity and obscurity, sinfulness and goodness. The dead leaves and mud are also part of the well. When we find ourselves trapped in it, we don't need to panic. We need to shift the focus of our consciousness from our immediate stuck-in-the-mud state to the truth that we do live and move and have our being in God, who is always greater than our subjective states.

Let us suppose, for example, that I have decided to start praying regularly. When I make this decision, I am in touch with the fine point of my soul, and I feel peaceful and sure that this is the right decision. I begin to put it into practice. Sooner or later the inner opposition will begin. "I could turn into a religious fanatic." "I'm too tired. I'll start the regular prayer when work pressure lessens." "*Laborare est orare*, 'work is prayer,' and this formal praying doesn't seem to be accomplishing anything for me." The conflict has begun. If I keep to my original decision, I shall experience peace in spite of the conflict. If I go with the opposition and abandon the prayer, I may experience immediate relief, but it will not last, and I shall feel uneasy. Directing your being toward God is never quite as simple as I have described it, but the guideline will help to some extent.

2. *If the core of your being is turned away from God, any decisions you make that are in harmony with that fundamental choice will comfort and console you,*

*while the creative forces outside and within you will
trouble you with stings of conscience.*

If my fundamental aim in life is that creation should praise,
reverence, and serve me, that I should focus my attention
on my aggrandizement, security, and importance, however
obtained and at whatever cost to others, then I shall welcome and delight in whatever furthers this fundamental
desire. Those who do not give me the attention I desire
will be hurtful and annoying to me, and I shall particularly
dislike and be pained by those who appear to be both
generous and happy. This second guideline can cause
anxiety, for how can you be sure that you are not funda-
mentally turned away from God? A good general rule is
always to give yourself the benefit of the doubt. Besides,
the very fact that you are anxious is a sign that the core of
your being is directed toward God; otherwise you would
not be worried, nor would you be reading this book.

Note that these two guidelines are not saying, "Nice
feelings are of God and nasty feelings are of the devil."
Feelings in themselves are neither good nor bad, but they
are indicators of what is healthy and unhealthy in us. Jesus
felt sadness: "My soul is sorrowful to the point of death"
(Matthew 26:38). He felt anger when he drove out the
dealers in the temple. He felt irritation with his disciples:
"Do you not yet understand? Have you no perception?
Are your minds closed?" (Mark 8:17). His sadness, anger,
and irritation sprang from his at-one-ness with God
encountering the obstinate alienation from God that
those around him were feeling. I may glow with self-
satisfaction at having demolished someone in an argument,
but this nice feeling indicates a perverse tendency.

3. *Distinguish creative moods and feelings from destructive ones not by their pleasantness or painfulness but by their effect. If going with your moods or feelings leads to an increase of faith, hope, and love, then they are creative; if it leads to a decrease of faith, hope, and love, then they are destructive.*

Suppose you have been unjustly treated. It is natural and healthy to feel angry. Anger in itself is not necessarily destructive; it may be very creative. God is frequently described as angry in the Scriptures, and the Old Testament prophets spoke angrily. Jesus, as recorded in Matthew 23, was angry with the Pharisees, whom he described as a brood of vipers, and he was so angry with the temple dealers that he drove them out of the temple with a whip. What you need to find out is where the emotion is coming from and where it is leading. Is the anger you experience leading you into total preoccupation with your own hurt, to the point of plotting vengeance and doing everything in your power to damage those who have hurt you, so that you are consumed with resentment? Or is your anger energizing you to oppose injustice, not just on your own behalf but on behalf of all its victims? The anger may make you reflect on the injustice you inflict on others. Or it may help you realize that the root of much of your anger may be your own violence toward yourself, such as when you try to force yourself to live according to other people's expectations and in the process stifle your true self. The anger in these last situations is creative. Frequently we are taught to believe that good Christians should never experience feelings of anger, irritation, sadness, inner darkness, or doubt, and if we do, we are taught to ignore them. But if ignored, they do not simply disappear; they go underground, spread their infection, and then reappear in much less obvious but more damaging forms, often in a general listlessness that leads to depression.

4. *Moods and inner feelings, whether nice or nasty, that draw us toward God are called "consolation." Painful moods and inner feelings that draw us away from God are called "desolation."*

Notice that consolation can feel either pleasant or painful, but desolation always feels painful. Desolation is possible only if the core of our being is centered on God. The pain comes from the inner conflict between this core movement toward God and the movement of the destructive spirit within and outside us. Therefore, to experience the pain of desolation is a good sign—like when the invalid starts to complain about feeling hungry.

Desolation is a mood with an inner dynamic that if followed will prove destructive; consolation is a mood with an inner dynamic that is creative. Desolation turns us in on ourselves so that we become preoccupied with our own kingdom and believe that we should be praised, reverenced, and served. Consolation, on the other hand, turns us outward so that we become more interested in life outside us, more capable of noticing other people, more able to share their joys and feel for them in their suffering, more inclined to pray.

We are not necessarily responsible for the moods that afflict us. What is important is how we respond to these moods. If we go with a destructive mood, it will damage others and ourselves; if we act against the mood, it will benefit everyone, including ourselves.

5. *In desolation, never go back on a decision you made in a time of consolation.*

The thoughts and judgments that spring from desolation are the opposite of those that spring from consolation. While you should never go back on a decision you made in a time of consolation, it is useful to act against the desolation. You should also examine the cause of your desolation.

Desolation can take different forms, so there will be different ways of acting against it. This is illustrated in the following scale:

0 1 2 3 4 5 6 7 8 9 10

0 = Deepest depression. I have no hope, no trust, and no love, and suicide seems to be the only way out.

10 = Manic activity. I am so active that I am like a fly-wheel that has lost its axis and is hurtling toward a break-down, at which point I revert to 0.

5 = The center point. The core of my being is centered on God and I experience inner harmony and peace.

4 and 6 = I experience normal and healthy fluctuations of mood that do not throw me off center.

3 through 1 = I am moving toward depression.

7 through 9 = I am moving toward hyperactivity.

Zero through 3 and 7 through 10 are states of desolation, for I am immersed either in my own feelings of hopelessness or my own hyperactivity. In either state, my judgment is impaired, my mind blinkered by my own immediate state, so I am in no position to make a clear decision.

Notice that the rule does not say that you should never make a decision in a time of desolation, only that you should not go back on a decision you made in a time of consolation. I may, for example, decide in consolation to join some voluntary organization or apply for a particular job. Then, in desolation, I may begin to doubt my original decision, feel disinclined to pray, and worry about the financial consequences of changing jobs. This guideline tells me not go back on my decision while I am in a state of desolation. Only later, when consolation has returned, can I decide to go back on my decision.

It is, however, useful to act against the desolation. How you act against it depends on the nature of the desolation. If you are caught between 0 and 3, then acting against it would demand a little more exertion—praying a bit more, deliberately reaching out more to others—whereas if you are between 7 and 10, acting against the desolation would mean giving yourself more rest—deliberately cutting down on activity even if it means cutting down on the time you give to prayer.

Examine the causes of your desolation. It may be a result of overworking yourself, which means that you need to be kinder to yourself, take more rest or more physical exercise if the work is mental, and take more time for meals and relaxation. Or your desolation may be a result of idleness and a preoccupation with your own immediate comfort, in which case you need to bestir yourself.

A frequent cause of desolation is in our relations with other people. If we harbor grudges and relish harm done to others, then it is not surprising that we cannot meet in prayer the God of forgiveness, tenderness, and compassion.

6. *In desolation, remember two things.*

Although you may feel as though desolation is a permanent state, know that it will pass.

Also remember that if you can keep the focus of your attention on God, even if you have no felt experience of his presence, he will teach you through the desolation. He will free you of your false securities and reveal himself to your own inner emptiness so that he may fill and possess it.

As we have seen, desolation can be a good sign, and it also can be very creative if we can react to it in faith. Take an extreme example of a woman who feels that she has lost everything: marriage, health, financial security, and reputation. Everything on which she relied for her security has been taken from her. The loss is leading her to despair, but if she can keep the core of her being centered on God, then she can come to know with her whole being and not just with her head that God really is her rock, refuge, and strength. Such knowledge is true humility, the source of all other virtues, a realization of the first of the beatitudes: "Blessed are those who really know their need of God; theirs is the kingdom of heaven." In all adversity, if we can see it in faith, God is nudging us toward the truth of things: that he is God and that our ultimate security, freedom, and peace are in him alone.

7. *In consolation, make the most of it.*

Acknowledge consolation as a freely given gift that reveals a deeper truth to your existence, namely, that you live always enfolded within the goodness and faithfulness of God. In consolation you have a felt experience of this truth, which can become the anchor of your hope in times of desolation.

These guidelines have dwelt so much on desolation that you may think that desolation is the Christian's normal state. It is not. Consolation should be the normal state, but we can be led astray if we do not understand that desolation afflicts us all at some time or another and that it must be interpreted correctly in order to be effectively countered.

We can be dangerously skeptical about feelings, which can lead us to ignore and discount them altogether. By doing this, we ignore and discount the gentle drawing of God. Felt consolation, especially if it is intense, does not usually last long. The feeling is not God's presence, for his presence is there always, "closer to me than I am to myself," but it is a sign of the reality in which we live. We live enfolded in his goodness not through any merit of our own but through a gift freely given to us. In consolation we need to pray that our felt knowledge of his goodness and closeness becomes a permanent knowledge, sustaining us even when we are deprived of the feelings.

8. *Face the fears that haunt you.*

The most destructive force within us is a mixture of fear plus imagination. Once they both break loose in us, the damage they can do is endless; together they form a force that robs us of our trust in God, in others, and in ourselves so that self-protection becomes the dominating desire of our lives and we end up locked in our own prison. It is striking that the most common phrase uttered by God in the Scriptures is "Do not be afraid," which is said to appear 365 times. The next most common phrase is "I am with you." If fears are not acknowledged, they go underground in our minds, spread, infect every aspect of our lives, and diminish us. Once acknowledged and faced, they have less of a hold on us. Very often the things we most fear are the things we most need, aspects of ourselves that we are afraid to acknowledge but without which we cannot find wholeness. Most of us cannot cope with our fears on our own, and so it is wise to talk about them with someone who will not judge us or overwhelm us with advice but will allow us to accept our fears and learn for ourselves what they are telling us.

God is the God of consolation. A useful summary of these rules for discernment is in the phrase "God draws; the destructive spirit drives" or "God is gentle; the evil spirit is violent." In Scripture the devil is called "the accuser." God's Spirit is called "the Paraclete," the advocate, the defender. Many Christians suffer from a permanent state of guilt, constantly accusing themselves or feeling that God is accusing them. Christ becomes an abstract ideal of selflessness, heroism, total generosity, honesty, and love. As we never reach that level, we feel that we are constant failures and hypocrites, the kind of lukewarm people of which the Book of Revelation speaks, fit only to be spat out of God's mouth. Our minds are haunted by "oughts," our spirits exhausted by trying to match up to them and tormented by their failure to do so. Whatever we do, we feel we should be doing something else; whatever we enjoy, we feel we should not be enjoying it; however we pray, we feel we should be able to pray better.

God is always gentle and attractive even when he is demanding. Rather than goad us from without, he prompts us from within. He encourages and excuses us, is patient and kind, trusts and never rejects us, knows our weaknesses and shares them, and never demands more of us than we are capable of giving. Dr. Frank Lake wrote of a spiritual disease called "hardening of the oughteries." It is good to examine the oughts in our lives. Are they coming from without or from within? Are they pointing to something that you want to do, even though it may be demanding, or something that you are not inclined to do but feel you ought to do? If the latter, then resist it. Pray to want it, if it is something good, but do not force yourself to do it.

The gospel is demanding, but God is always gentle. Jesus said, "The kingdom of heaven is like a mustard seed which a man took and sowed in his field. It is the smallest of all the seeds" (Matthew 13:31–32). Our growth in God is slow and gradual. "Can any of you, for all his worrying, add a single cubit to his span of life?" (Luke 12:25). We must not expect to reach holiness in a day. Another important parable is that of the Pharisee and the tax collector who went up to the temple to pray. The Pharisee, like the sheepdog, was an excellent performer, fasting twice a week and giving tithes of all he possessed, but his attention was focused on himself and his achievements. The tax collector was a pathetic performer and had broken all the commandments, but he acknowledged his own helplessness. His attention was focused on God, and his prayer was "Be merciful to me, a sinner" (Luke 18:13). Jesus says that it was the tax collector who left the temple in a right relationship with God. However you pray, keep the fine point of your soul focused on God even when your mind is distracted and your heart heavy.

Here is an exercise that you may find helpful.

A DAILY EXERCISE: REVIEW OF THE DAY

God is in the facts, so there must be kindness in the facts, however disastrous they may appear to us. It is in the events of each day that we are to find God. This exercise is a way of recognizing God's beckoning and our response.

- Relax and pray, "Lord, let my whole being be directed to your service and praise."

- Replay the day, in any order. Look first at those moments you have enjoyed. Relive them, relish them, and thank God for them. They are his gift to you. Avoid any self-judgment.

- Now pray for enlightenment, "Lord, that I may see." Notice your moods and inner feelings during the day without judging them. Moods and inner feelings arise from our desires. Our habitual desires become attitudes. When our desires/attitudes are satisfied, we are content; when they are frustrated, we become irritable. We are praying to know the desires and attitudes that underlie our moods. Are my desires/attitudes directed to his kingdom—am I living to praise, reverence, and serve God?—or are my desires/attitudes directed to my personal kingdom—my comfort, wealth, status, success, honor? Do I want creation to praise, reverence, and serve me?

- Apologize to God for not responding to him during the events of the day and beg his forgiveness, knowing that he always gives it. Thank him too for the times you have responded.

- Ask God for his guidance for tomorrow and entrust yourself to his goodness like a child in its mother's arms (Psalm 131:2).

Chapter 5

Writing a Faith Autobiography

MY EDITORS INVITED ME TO ADD A NOTE TO THIS BOOK ON keeping a spiritual journal. As I have never succeeded in keeping a spiritual journal for more than a few spasmodic months at a time, I declined the invitation. Instead, I offer these notes on writing your own faith autobiography. The method is very simple and well suited to the ill disciplined, for it does not have to be done regularly each day.

METHOD

Ask yourself the question "What have been the key events in my life: the people, places, ideas?" Briefly scribble down whatever occurs to you; you do not have to recall events chronologically. Even if you spend only a short time on this exercise, you will soon discover the linked nature of your memories. Once you have deliberately recalled a few events, others will begin to pop into your consciousness. Add them to your list. It is important that you do not deliberately indulge in any analysis or moralizing at this stage or in any self-approval or disapproval; you are simply recalling events. In your writings, do not worry about style, grammar, or spelling. Write freely and for your eyes only.

Even if you do this exercise on only one occasion, it will be helpful. If you would like to continue with it, take a further step by recalling memories that linger, especially memories from childhood, no matter how trivial they may seem. The fact that they linger in your memory is a sign that they are important. Scribble down not just the events themselves but the emotions you had at the time, as far as you can remember them.

While on a sabbatical recently, I began this process of recalling memories that linger, however insignificant they appeared. At first I was tempted to abandon the work, for it seemed to be a fruitless indulgence, but I soon began to make new discoveries.

One discovery was about the nature of memory. We tend to think of memory as an office for our personal records, its files supplying information about past events, but memory is much more like an arsenal than an archive. Our memories may be compared to energy charges within us, the energy being either creative or destructive. The creative/destructive quality depends not only on the original event but also on the way we now view it. For example, an experience of rejection in childhood, whether real or imagined, can affect our attitude toward all future relationships, leaving us fearful of further rejection and distrustful of any close relationship. The original event may no longer be in our conscious memory, but its effects remain. By recalling the original event and bringing it before God in prayer, we can begin to see it in a broader perspective. God was, is, and always will be our rock, refuge, and strength. The sense of rejection, which had been so destructive, now leads us into a deeper appreciation and awareness of God's enveloping and supporting presence at all times so that what had been a deadening experience now becomes life giving.

Another discovery I made was about the sequence of events in life, the apparent coincidences, the interconnectedness of things, and the importance and value of periods in my life that at the time seemed a waste. This exercise in pondering memories that linger helped me to see much more clearly that we are all caught up in a life that is far greater than our conscious minds can grasp. I found this a very freeing and energizing experience.

Where does faith come in?

In describing the method, I have deliberately made no explicit mention of faith because we can find God only in and through our own experience. The God of Abraham, Isaac, and Jacob, the Father of our Lord, Jesus Christ, is the same God who is now holding us in being. We read the Scriptures in order to recognize that same God now working within us, bringing us out of the land of Egypt, through the wilderness, and into the Promised Land. Through the faith autobiography the Scriptures will become more alive to us, and we will begin to feel a real kinship with the characters, good and bad, that appear in them. The God of the Scriptures will be "closer to me than I am to myself," writing further volumes in our lives, still hovering over the chaos, bringing order and life out of the most unpromising material. "Glory be to him whose power, working in us, can do infinitely more than we can ask or imagine" (Ephesians 3:20).

PART TWO

REFLECTIONS FOR THE SOUL

Sunday

JOURNEY

Ephesians 1:3–8

Before the world was made, [God] chose us, chose us in Christ, to be holy and spotless, and to live through love in his presence, determining that we should become his adopted sons [and daughters], through Jesus Christ for his own kind purposes, to make us praise the glory of his grace, his free gift to us in the Beloved, in whom, through his blood, we gain our freedom, the forgiveness of our sins. Such is the richness of the grace which he has showered on us in all wisdom and insight.

EPHESİAПS I:4–8

Reading Scripture helps us recognize God at work in our own lives now. The God of Abraham, Isaac, and Jacob, the God of St. Paul, the God of our Lord, Jesus Christ, is the God now holding us in being.

The language of Scripture can seem very remote from us. "God chose us in Christ to be holy and spotless, and to live through love in his presence." Do those words answer, as the Quakers would say, to your condition? Do

89

you ever feel frustrated, useless, empty, hopeless? Do you ever feel that your life has no meaning or purpose? And do those feelings cause you pain? When you are in that state of mind, if someone were to tell you, "Cheer up. Before the world was made God chose you, chose you in Christ, to be holy and spotless, and to live through love in his presence," would his or her words seem empty, a mockery, worthy only of a hollow laugh in response?

These moods of hopelessness are in reality full of hope and promise. The pain you feel is a good sign, for it means that something in you is rebelling against your sense of hopelessness and meaninglessness.

Going on a pilgrimage is an ancient and widespread custom. Pilgrimages have been described as the poor person's substitute for mysticism. Our inner life, if we dare to look at it, is very complex: we are full of hopes and fears and longings. One way of dealing with this inner complexity is to externalize it. We choose some holy spot that corresponds to our inner longings and then walk toward it. It is surprising how much of our inner complexity unravels in the process. We begin to realize, for example, that our pilgrimage destination is a factor in every decision we make along the way: the direction we take, the luggage we carry, how long we stay in each place. It is the destination that gives meaning to the journey.

Few of us have the time, money, or energy to go on long walking pilgrimages, but all of us are on a journey through life, whether we like it or not. If we have no idea of the direction in which we're going, then our journey is bound to appear meaningless.

How can we find direction? We can begin by listening to our own inner longings. A useful way of doing this is to imagine that you have died. Write your own obituary, but not the one you are afraid you will receive. Instead, write the obituary that in your wildest dreams you would love to have, not letting reality limit you in the slightest. This imaginative exercise can put you in touch with new depths of yourself. Your ultimate identity is in God. No matter how bad you may feel about yourself, you are called to become the goodness of God. Focus your attention on this dream, and your heart will begin to know that this is not an empty dream but the truth of things. This will become your destination and will determine every choice you make on your journey through life.

Prayer

> *God, before the world was, you had me in mind, and you created me as a unique manifestation of yourself. Show me your attractiveness, so that the one longing of my heart will be to let you be God to me and through me. Amen.*

Monday

LONGING

Psalm 42

*As a doe longs for running streams, so longs my soul for
you, my God. My soul thirsts for God, the God of life;
when shall I go to see the face of God? I have no food but
tears, day and night; and all day long men say to me,
"Where is your God?" I remember, and my soul melts
within me: I am on my way to the wonderful Tent.*

PSALM 42:1—4

The Psalms are full of longing for God. When I was
young, the Psalms bored me. I could not understand why
the psalmist was so enthusiastic about a God who was
invisible, intangible, remote, and threatening and who
appeared to be almost exclusively interested in our sins.
I could understand why "All day long men say to me,
'Where is your God?'"

We can meet God only within our own experience. Our
hearts are the compasses for our journey toward God.
What is it you long for? When we begin to ask ourselves
this question, we realize how difficult it is to answer. When

Jesus asked the Gerasene demoniac his name, he answered with great insight, "My name is legion because there are many of us." What is it you long for? When we begin to ask ourselves this question, we discover that our longings are legion and most of them conflicting. We want to be truthful and popular. We want to be open-minded, but we also long for certainty. We want to be gentle, but we also want to be in control of things. We want to be able to love, but we also like having our own way. By focusing on the question "What is it you long for?" we begin on our inner journey toward God.

Would you like to be a transparently honest person, totally true? Would you like to be able to love with your whole being, really wishing the good of the other as though you were wishing it for yourself? Would you like to have a passionate love for justice on behalf of others, no matter what it might cost you? Would you like to be a peacemaker, able to reconcile enemies? Would you like to be effectively compassionate so that your presence brings hope and comfort to others? Would you like to be an effective champion of the poor, oppressed, and downtrodden? In answering these questions, do not be put off by your lamentable performance in any of these areas. Answering yes to any of these questions is a sign of your longing for God, for God is truth and love, the God of compassion and justice, the God of the poor and oppressed. Remember the saying "The appetite grows by what it feeds on." The more we can focus on these things for which we long, the stronger the longing will become, and the greater our loathing of whatever opposes that longing.

When we take a walking pilgrimage, we know that the luggage we carry is for the journey, so we travel as lightly as possible. We also know that the more fussy we are about the weather, the more miserable the journey is likely to be, because it will almost always be too hot, too cold, too windy, or too wet. We know that we just have to accept the weather as it is, and when we do, the journey becomes easier. We know too that on a walking pilgrimage, the more wedded we are to what is familiar to us, the more threatening we will find everything that is new. Thus our pilgrimage through strange countries, where we will meet foreign people who have different customs and beliefs from us, will be an unpleasant and frightening experience. The more we can be like the Latin poet Terence, who wrote "Nothing that is human is foreign to me," the more interesting and enjoyable the journey will be.

But in ordinary life, we easily forget these obvious truths. We conduct our lives as though the journey were for the sake of the luggage: I have, therefore I am. Much of our misery comes from our fixed expectations because nothing is ever right. When we let go of our expectations, we are freed of an enormous burden.

Prayer

> *God, help me to recognize the world as your sacrament—as a sign, an effective sign, of your presence in all things and all people.*

Tuesday

JUDGING

Luke 5:6–11

And when they had done this they netted such a huge number
of fish that their nets began to tear, so they signaled to their
companions in the other boat to come and help them; when
these came, they filled the two boats to sinking point.

    When Simon Peter saw this he fell at the knees of Jesus
saying, "Leave me, Lord; I am a sinful man." For he and
all his companions were completely overcome by the catch
they had made. . . . But Jesus said to Simon, "Do not be
afraid; from now on it is men you will catch." Then,
bringing their boats back to land, they left everything and
followed him.

LUKE 5:6—11

Peter's reaction to the miraculous draft of fish is revealing.
He is at first overwhelmed by the catch, but his attention
immediately reverts to himself and his sinfulness, so he says,
"Leave me, Lord." Jesus' answer is "Do not be afraid," and
Peter's response is to leave everything and follow Jesus.

    If we believe that God's words are being spoken to us

when we pray the Scriptures, our reaction may be like Peter's: "Leave me, for I am sinful." Or our reaction may not be as explicit as Peter's; instead of telling God to leave us, we may be so preoccupied with our own sense of failure or inadequacy that we cannot even attend to God's invitation. Or we may be people of such sound common sense that we ignore our deepest longings and dreams and plod on through life with visionless eyes, our love of common sense blighting our lives.

St. Paul, in his prayers for the Ephesians, writes, "Out of his infinite glory, may he give you the power through his Spirit for your hidden self to grow strong, so that Christ may live in your hearts through faith. . . . [God's] power, working in us, can do infinitely more than we can ask or imagine" (Ephesians 3:16–17, 20).

God's goodness is much more powerful than our sinfulness. That is why it is so important for us to keep the focus of our attention on God's goodness rather than on our own sinfulness or, still worse, other people's. This is not to deny the reality of sin in ourselves or in others but to forbid our sins to determine the direction of our lives. Our destination in life's journey is to share the life of God, not to wallow in our own and the world's sinfulness.

Jesus does not deny Peter's unworthiness. He knows it better than Peter, but still he says, "Do not be afraid." And he says the same to us. It is not our virtue that brings us to our destination but the goodness of God. The tax gatherer, who is at the bottom of the virtue charts, not the Pharisee, who is number one, comes out of the Temple in a right relationship with God. The tax gatherer, aware of his own faults, entrusts himself to God's goodness, while the Pharisee is too full of his own goodness to recognize God's.

When you focus your attention on God's goodness and your own deepest longings in prayer, notice afterward the effect this has on you. Does life seem more interesting, less burdensome, and more enjoyable? Are you becoming more aware of other people and things? What are the effects of not focusing your attention on God's goodness and instead being preoccupied with your own failures and inadequacy, both in prayer and out of it? Do you feel even heavier, more hopeless, engrossed in your own shortcomings? These feelings are God's nudgings, encouraging you to look toward God's goodness, not to your own performance.

In the Jerusalem Bible, the Book of Wisdom contains the lines "You [God] . . . overlook men's sins so that they can repent" (Wisdom 11:24). The Authorized Version of the Apocrypha uses the delightful translation "He winketh at our sins, so that we may amend"!

Prayer

> *God, I beg you, keep nudging me until I know at every level of my being that you are my rock, my refuge, my strength, and my joy. Amen.*

Wednesday

REPENTANCE

Joel 2:12–18; 2 Corinthians 5:20–6:2;
Matthew 6:1–6, 16–18

Let your hearts be broken, not your garments torn, turn
to Yahweh your God again, for he is all tenderness and
compassion, slow to anger, rich in graciousness and ready
to relent.

JOEL 2:13

For our sake God made the sinless one into sin, so that in
him we might become the goodness of God.

2 CORINTHIANS 5:21

Be careful not to parade your good deeds before men to
attract their notice. . . . And when you pray, do not imitate
the hypocrites: they love to say their prayers standing up in
the synagogues and at the street corners for people to see
them. . . . When you fast do not put on a gloomy look as
the hypocrites do: they pull long faces to let men know they
are fasting.

MATTHEW 6:1, 5, 16

"When a man knows he is to be hanged in a fortnight, it concentrates his mind wonderfully," wrote Dr. Johnson. In the early days of Christianity, ashes were placed on the heads of penitents at the start of Lent, when they began to prepare for their return to the church on Maundy Thursday. Today the ceremony is offered to all Christians. The imposition of ashes is accompanied with the words "Remember, thou art dust and unto dust thou shalt return," words that, if we let them in, can also wonderfully concentrate the mind.

As a university chaplain, I placed ashes on the foreheads of hundreds of healthy-looking students, most of them grinning at this quaint ceremony. They were right to smile. "Dust to dust" is not the whole truth, but it is a useful part to remember when we find ourselves preoccupied with our looks, health, success, wealth, and status. Remembering that we are from dust and are dust destined can free us from much useless anxiety and allow us to see the funny side of ourselves and of others.

But what is the point of this brief interlude between states of dust? "Before the world was made, he chose us, chose us in Christ . . . to live through love in his presence" (Ephesians 1:4). Life in the body is a stage on our journey but such an important and precious stage that God himself, in Jesus, joined us on the journey, died, and is risen again "so that in him we might become the goodness of God," as Paul says. How are we to become the goodness of God? By letting God be God to us and through us. So "Love your enemies, do good to those who hate you. . . . Be compassionate as your Father is compassionate" (Luke 6:27, 36).

When we look at our lives and preoccupations individually, as a church, and as a nation in the light of the words

"Love your enemies, do good to those who hate you,"
then we can begin to understand Joel's cry of "Let your
hearts be broken, not your garments torn, turn to Yahweh
your God again, for he is all tenderness and compassion."

As we have seen, we can turn back to God through
prayer, fasting, and almsdeeds. In today's gospel, Jesus tells
us to do all three quietly and without ostentation. "Put oil
on your head and wash your face, so that no one will know
you are fasting" (Matthew 6:17).

In your own prayer today, focus your attention on the
moments of your life for which you are grateful. Thank
God for them, talk to him about them, and beg him to
teach you to treat others as God has treated you. Pray to
know God's tenderness and compassion in those moments
too for which you do not feel at all grateful at the time.

Prayer

> *O God, Father and Mother of all, from whom we come
> and to whom we go, enlighten our minds and hearts, so
> that in recognizing your goodness in our own lives we may
> become your goodness. We ask you this through Jesus
> Christ, our Lord. Amen.*

Thursday

CHOOSING LIFE

*Deuteronomy 30:15–20; Luke 9:22–25;
Psalm 1*

*[Moses said to the people], "See, today I set before you life
and prosperity, death and disaster. . . . I set before you life
or death, blessing or curse. Choose life, then, so that you
and your descendants may live, in the love of Yahweh your
God, obeying his voice, clinging to him; for in this your life
consists, and on this depends your long stay in the land
which Yahweh swore to your fathers Abraham, Isaac and
Jacob he would give them."*

DEUTERONOMY 30:15, 19–20

*Then he said to them all, "If any want to become my fol-
lowers, let them deny themselves and take up their cross
daily and follow me. For those who want to save their life
will lose it, and those who lose their life for my sake will
save it. What does it profit them if they gain the whole
world, but lose or forfeit themselves?"*

LUKE 9:23–25, NRSV

Moses gave the Israelites this message on their journey through the wilderness. The same message is being given to us on our journey, though "Choose life, not death" may seem to be an unnecessary piece of advice. People don't usually choose death intentionally.

A useful exercise for you to do involves taking a piece of paper and dividing it into two columns, one headed "Events that bring me to life" and the other "Events that deaden me." Then scribble down whatever comes to mind. Keep the list and add to it whenever another item occurs to you. If you persist, the list will lengthen, and you may discover that you give more time and attention to the things that deaden you than to those that enliven you.

It is also good to reflect on your list in light of the statement "We are created to praise, reverence, and serve God." For each item on your list ask yourself, "Is it this that brings me to life, or do I come to life only when creation is praising, reverencing, and serving me? Does everything that is not praising me or promoting my self-importance, comfort, and security deaden me?" This self-centeredness is the way of death; God-centeredness is the way of life. Jesus says this in Luke 9:23–25 (NRSV): "If any want to become my followers, let them deny themselves and take up their cross daily and follow me. For those who want to save their life will lose it, and those who lose their life for my sake will save it. What does it profit them if they gain the whole world, but lose or forfeit themselves?"

"If anyone wants to be a follower of mine, let them renounce themselves." Taken out of context, these words have caused havoc in many Christians' lives because they focus attention on renunciation as though it were something good in itself. In this light, God is seen as being most pleased with us when we are giving ourselves a hard time, and our holiness is measured by our ability to endure suffering. This is a total distortion of Jesus' message. The renunciation that he demands is a renunciation of all those things that deaden us so that we may live more fully. To live more fully we must free ourselves from self-preoccupation so that we can delight in his creation, know ourselves as at one with it, and see our lives as a gift given to us so that others may live more fully. Therefore, we should look carefully at and ensure that we give time to our list of events that bring us to life and help us appreciate, value, cherish, and wonder at God's creation.

Find a line or two in the reading that directs your attention to your longing for life, such as "Choose life, then, so that you and your descendants may live in the love of Yahweh your God," and speak to God from your heart, telling him of your longings and asking him to guide you. "God, create a clean heart in me, put into me a new and constant spirit" (Psalm 51:10).

Prayer

> *God, source of all life, Power of all power, in whom we live and move and have our being, release us from our imprisoning fears and from every form of self-preoccupation, which rob us of the gift of wonder at the miracles of your creation and blind us to you, present in all things and dwelling in every human being. We ask you this through Jesus Christ, our Lord. Amen.*

Friday

FASTING

Isaiah 58:1–9; Psalm 51; Matthew 9:14–15

Look, you do business on your fast days,
you oppress all your workmen;
look, you quarrel and squabble when you fast
and strike the poor man with your fist.
Fasting like yours today
will never make your voice heard on high.
Is that the sort of fast that pleases me,
a truly penitential day for men? . . .
Is not this the sort of fast that pleases me
—it is the Lord Yahweh who speaks—
to break unjust fetters
and undo the thongs of the yoke,
to let the oppressed go free,
and break every yoke,
to share your bread with the hungry,
and shelter the homeless poor,
to clothe the man you see to be naked
and not turn from your own kin?

*Then will your light shine like the dawn
and your wound be quickly healed over.*

ISAIAH 58:3—8

This passage illustrates very clearly the meaning of fasting.
Fasting is not an end in itself but a means to an end. The
end is becoming more sensitive to the reality of God, a
God of mercy and compassion who loves all his creation
and is within and among us. Our lives should mirror the
compassion of God. Fidelity to the covenant does not
consist primarily in observing religious fasts and rituals
but also in letting God be God in us and through us in all
our relations with other people, no matter who they are.

In the above reading, Isaiah is addressing a very devout
people. They pray and fast regularly, but their devotions
and fasting are abhorrent to God because their religious
words and gestures do not correspond to their lives.

We read Scripture in the belief that through the medium
of its message, God is still speaking to us now. While most
of us do not go around punching the poor, holding people
captive, or oppressing workers, neither, most likely, did the
majority of those Isaiah was addressing. Prophetic messages
are never directed to individuals but always to the nation,
and if an individual is addressed, it is only because he or
she is a representative of the nation. The message today
might read:

Look, you vote for whatever politicians will give the
wealthier among you an extra penny on the dollar at the
expense of the suffering poor in your midst.

Look, on your fast day you launch furnace-throwing
monsters, threatening all life on earth.

Look, you cut down on aid for those nations whose
wealth you yourselves have plundered.

Look, you prostitute yourselves to market forces, neglecting your own homeless poor and rendering the poor person helpless.

When we look at the problems of injustice, world hunger, homelessness, violence, the arms trade, and the threat of nuclear defense systems to human existence, we may feel overwhelmed by the enormity of the problems and our own helplessness to effect any change. We need to stay focused on our helplessness until we realize that we are leaving out God, "whose power, working in us, can do infinitely more than we can ask or imagine" (Ephesians 3:20).

Prayer

> *God, lover of all that you have created, whose living Spirit is in all, melt down the defenses of our minds and hearts with the waves of your compassion, so that by surrendering to you we may be delivered from our imprisoning self-interest into the expanse of your kingdom. We ask you this through Jesus Christ, our Lord. Amen.*

Saturday

SIN

Isaiah 58:9–14; Psalm 86; Luke 5:27–32

If you do away with the yoke,
the clenched fist, the wicked word,
if you give your bread to the hungry,
and relief to the oppressed,
your light will rise in the darkness. . . .
Yahweh will always guide you,
giving you relief in desert places. . . .
and you shall be like a watered garden,
like a spring of water
whose waters never run dry.

ISAIAH 58:9–11

[Jesus] noticed a tax collector, Levi by name, sitting by the customs house, and said to him, "Follow me." And leaving everything he got up and followed him. In his honor Levi held a great reception in his house. . . . The Pharisees and their scribes complained to his disciples and said, "Why do you eat and drink with tax collectors and sinners?" Jesus said to them in reply, "It is not those who are well who need

the doctor, but the sick. I have not come to call the virtuous,
but sinners to repentance."

The prophets did not spare their people; they flayed them
with their denunciations. They did so not because they
delighted in being cruel but to bring the people back to
life: "You shall be like a spring of water."

Levi is a despicable character: he collects taxes to be
paid to the occupying Romans and lines his own pocket
too. Today his equivalent might be a drug pusher who
makes money out of the misery of others.

These two passages reveal to us the difference between
God and ourselves. We take great delight in scandal,
provided we are clear of it ourselves. The tabloids entertain
millions and make millions by exposing the sins of public
figures. They add to the effect by denouncing and
humiliating the wrongdoers from a great height of moral
righteousness and then suggesting suitably severe punish-
ments. Anyone who sympathizes with these victims is
described as a "wimp," "spineless," or "lacking moral fiber."
According to the description of God in the Bible, he would
deserve all these epithets.

It is a useful and sobering exercise to make a list of all
those things you most despise in other people. When the
list is complete, treasure it, because it is almost certainly
describing those characteristics in yourself that you are
least willing to admit you possess. Psychologists call this
"projection" because you are projecting onto others those
aspects of yourself that you dislike, have disowned, or are
ashamed of. We usually project unconsciously, and thus
inwardly we feel full of self-righteousness as we denounce
the evils of other people. In this respect, we are like the

108 | SEVEN WEEKS FOR THE SOUL

tabloid journalists and are worthy successors of the Pharisees in the Gospels.

Seraphim of Sarov, a nineteenth-century Russian mystic, once wrote, "All condemnation is of the devil. Never condemn each other. Not even those whom you catch at the evil deed. We condemn others only because we shun knowing ourselves. When we gaze at our own failings, we see such a morass of filth that nothing in another can equal it. That is why we turn away and make much of the faults of others."

If we recognize our sins and weaknesses, God will always welcome us back. In fact, he says, "I have not come to call the virtuous, but sinners to repentance" (Luke 5:32).

Prayer

> *Deliver us, Lord, from every form of self-righteousness and every trace of satisfaction in our condemnation of one another. Show us our own sinfulness so that we, knowing the depths of your forgiveness and the tenderness of your love, may bear witness to your loving mercy in all our dealings. We ask you this through Jesus Christ, our Lord. Amen.*

Sunday

THE TEMPTATIONS OF ADAM AND JESUS

Genesis 3:1–7; Romans 5:12–19; Matthew 4:1–11

Then the serpent said to the woman, "No! You will not die! God knows in fact that on the day you eat it your eyes will be opened and you will be like gods, knowing good and evil."

GENESIS 3:4–5

Then Jesus was led by the Spirit out into the wilderness to be tempted by the devil. He fasted for forty days and forty nights, after which he was very hungry, and the tempter came and said to him, "If you are the Son of God, tell these stones to turn into loaves." But he replied, "Scripture says: 'Man does not live on bread alone but on every word that comes from the mouth of God.'"

MATTHEW 4:1–4

Whether we believe in the devil or not, we all will be confronted with the problem of evil and will search for a solution to it. The description of the Fall in the Book of

Genesis is Israel's answer to the problem. The Israelites' more prosperous and powerful neighbors had a variety of explanations for evil, all of which exonerated the individual from any evil that he or she might do and blamed the gods, who had either made the individual evil or had prompted him or her to perform particular evil acts. Religion was concerned with keeping on the right side of warring gods, placating them with suitable offerings, which might include human sacrifices. Israel's answer to evil is that there is only one God, whose creation is good; that human beings, both men and women, are made in his image; and that evil is not outside us but within us. The serpent makes the suggestion, and Adam and Eve consent to it. Evil is conceived and born within the human heart.

The serpent's suggestion in the Garden is very reasonable. The first Adam accepts the serpent's suggestion; the second Adam rejects it. The devil's temptation in the desert is also quite reasonable: Why not accept what looks good and promises power, and why not turn stones into bread to satisfy our own and other people's hunger? Why are the temptations portrayed in this way—as being so subtle and so reasonable? It is because they are describing the nature of evil, which creeps up on us like a snake and offers us what appears to be good and reasonable.

It is good for us to care for our health. It is good for us to create and enjoy wealth, which is a form of energy. It is right for us to impose control in our society, for it would disintegrate without some form of law and order. It is right for us to try to develop our talents and abilities. However, if we pursue any of these good things for the benefit of ourselves, our group, or our nation and do so at the expense of other people, then the good we pursue becomes destructive, not only to others but also to ourselves. The twentieth century is full of terrifying examples of this truth. The Third Reich promised to restore Germany to greatness, and within a few years its dominion had spread from the channel ports to the Urals. The restoration brought death to twenty million Russians, six million Jews, and several million German and Allied troops. The evil infected the Allies, who then deliberately bombed innocent civilians, leaving most German cities in ruins.

How can we preserve ourselves against the subtleties and deceits of evil? By ourselves, we cannot. That is why we have to pray and submit ourselves to the word of God, allowing it to enlighten our minds and hearts and help us distinguish between what is creative and what is destructive within our own hearts. Then we can pursue what is creative, thanking God for it, and show him what is destructive, asking him to deliver us from it. He will rescue us from every evil, whether it is evil done to us or evil we have done. "If it is certain that death reigned over everyone as the consequence of one man's fall, it is even more certain that one man, Jesus Christ, will cause everyone to reign in life who receives the free gift that he does not deserve, of being made righteous" (Romans 5:17).

Prayer

> *Grant us, Lord, that as we contemplate Jesus' time in the desert our hearts and minds may be enlightened by his truth, so that we may recognize the deceits and lies of the Evil One, who is masquerading under the appearance of good in ourselves, in our churches, and in our nation. We ask you this through Jesus Christ, our Lord. Amen.*

Monday

THE HOLINESS OF GOD AND ISRAEL

Leviticus 19:1–2, 11–18; Psalm 19;
Matthew 25:31–46

Say to them: "Be holy, for I, Yahweh your God, am holy.
. . . You must not steal nor deal deceitfully or fraudulently
with your neighbor. . . . You must not exploit or rob your
neighbor. You must not keep back the laborer's wage until
next morning. . . . You must not be guilty of unjust verdicts.
You must neither be partial to the little man nor overawed
by the great. . . . You must not bear hatred for your brother
in your heart. . . . You must love your neighbor as yourself."

LEVITICUS 19:2, 11, 13, 15, 17–18

In so far as you did this [feeding the hungry, giving drink
to the thirsty, welcoming the stranger, clothing the naked,
visiting the sick and imprisoned] to one of the least . . . you
did it to me. . . . In so far as you neglected to do this to one
of the least of these, you neglected to do it to me.

MATTHEW 25:40, 45

When a person is described as being holy, it suggests to us that the person is withdrawn and impractical, someone who spends an inordinate amount of time praying and whose conversation is limited to pious reflections and exhortations, someone who has a minimal appetite and is given to tears. The picture reflects our own mistaken notion of what holiness means. Leviticus spells out the meaning of holiness: it is earthy, practical, wise, and can be practiced in any state of life. When Jesus describes the Final Judgment, he does not mention prayer, fasting, religious beliefs or rituals, or any kind of orthodoxy; he simply says that our relationship to God is in our relationship to our neighbor. Serving our neighbor is serving God; neglecting our neighbor is neglecting God. The message is clear, but we keep ignoring it, persisting in thinking that holiness is an individual matter, an attitude of mind and heart that is suitable for church services but quite impractical elsewhere.

God is holy. We have discussed two aspects of God's holiness: his transcendence and his immanence. God is transcendent, always beyond our thinking and imagining and separate and different from his creation, and he is immanent, in all things, "closer to me than I am to myself," as Augustine said. "In him we live, and move, and exist," said Paul. In his immanence, God is "tender and compassionate, slow to anger, most loving" (Psalm 103:8).

When God tells Moses to say to the people of Israel "Be holy, for I, the Lord your God, am holy," he means that Israel must keep itself separate from everything that is opposed to the holiness of God. Thus the first commandment is "You shall have no Gods except me." The people of Israel must never identify God with anything in creation.

They are called to be pilgrims, but their final destination is beyond this world. While they are in this world, their minds, hearts, and actions must reflect the immanent holiness of God, mirroring his tenderness, compassion, kindness, and faithfulness.

Prayer and fasting are of value only insofar as they help us keep our minds and hearts focused on God, the Holy One, so that we can become channels of his compassion for all creation. Holiness is not to be measured by the time we spend in prayer, nor by the visions, ecstasies, or inner feelings we may have, but by the quality of our relationships, how they reflect the goodness and love of God. Someone has written, "We are as near to God as we are to the person we like least." I have a horrible suspicion that the writer may be right.

Prayer

Spirit of God, Holy One, breathe your Spirit into us, so that safe from every form of idolatry our lives may mirror your tenderness and loving compassion for all creation. We ask you this through Jesus Christ, our Lord. Amen.

Tuesday

PRAYER

Isaiah 55:10–11; Psalm 34;
Matthew 6:7–15

In your prayers do not babble as the pagans do, for they think that by using many words they will make themselves heard. Do not be like them; your Father knows what you need before you ask him. So you should pray like this:

Our Father in heaven,
may your name be held holy,
your kingdom come,
your will be done,
on earth as in heaven.
Give us today our daily bread.
And forgive us our debts,
as we have forgiven those who are in debt to us.
And do not put us to the test,
but save us from the evil one.

MATTHEW 6:7–13

"Do not babble as the pagans do." We can babble the "Our Father" as well as any pagan. When we pray, we are all liable to a neurosis that compels us to enter into a praying endurance test, with our success measured by the number of words uttered. When it is over, we experience relief and hope that God is satisfied for the time being, as though he is a God who imposes prayer tariffs, sending down thunderbolts on all who do not pay up regularly. Prayer is for our benefit, not God's. He is not interested in our prayers, as the prophets make clear, except insofar as they are expressions of minds and hearts that are longing for him.

We can pray the "Our Father" in many ways. One method is to pray it in rhythm with our breathing, uttering a syllable, word, or phrase with each breath. Or we can pray it when we walk, saying a word or phrase with each step or each two or three steps. Rhythmic prayer can bring stillness. Stay with this stillness as long as you can and do not feel pressured to complete the whole prayer.

Another way of praying the "Our Father" is to dwell on each phrase for as long as you can, reflecting on it, repeating it slowly, and speaking to God in whatever way the phrase moves you to do.

"Our Father" (or Mother, if that is more helpful to you). When you say "Our," every other human being is your sister or brother. Pray for that sense of at-one-ness with friends and enemies, acquaintances and strangers.

"In heaven." God is transcendent, always greater, never to be identified exclusively with any particular theory, way of thinking, ideology, church, or nation. He is a beckoning God, and we are called to be a pilgrim people.

"May your name be held holy." May we never use you,

claiming that our self-centered interests are your will. May our lives reflect your love and tenderness.

"Your kingdom come." May we let your kingdom—a kingdom of justice, truth, and peace—reign within our own hearts, within our own immediate circles, within our own church and nation. Teach us to keep asking, in all our actions, attitudes, and feelings, "Whose kingdom am I promoting, mine or yours?"

"May your will be done." Help me to recognize your will in the circumstances of my life, to discern your nudgings in life's joys and sorrows, failures and successes. Help me to change the things I can change and accept the things I cannot change, and give me the wisdom to recognize the difference.

"Give us today our daily bread." Help us to live and act as stewards of all we possess so that we never deprive others of their daily bread. Deliver us all from the idolatry of consumerism.

"Forgive us our debts." Let us know of our need for your forgiveness so that we can discover the depths of your forgiving love toward us and so be enabled to forgive those who have wronged us.

Prayer

> *Father, Mother of us all, teach us to be patient in prayer and in life so that we can learn to see you in our darkness and hear you in the silence of our own emptiness. You are our light, our salvation, our God in whom we trust. We ask you this through Jesus Christ, our Lord. Amen.*

Wednesday

GOD'S MERCY FOR ALL CREATION

Jonah 3:1–10; Psalm 51; Luke 11:29–32

*The word of Yahweh was addressed a second time to Jonah:
"Up!" he said, "Go to Nineveh, the great city, and preach to
them." . . . Jonah went on into the city. . . . He preached in
these words, "Only forty days more and Nineveh is going to
be destroyed." And the people of Nineveh believed in God;
they proclaimed a fast and put on sackcloth, from the greatest
to the least. The news reached the king of Nineveh, who rose
from his throne, took off his robe, put on sackcloth and sat
down in ashes. A proclamation was then promulgated
throughout Nineveh. . . . "Men and beasts, herds and flocks,
are to taste nothing; they must not eat, they must not drink
water. All are to put on sackcloth and call on God with all
their might. . . . Who knows if God will not change his
mind and relent?" . . . God saw their efforts to renounce
their evil behavior. And God relented: he did not inflict on
them the disaster which he had threatened.*

JONAH 3:1–2, 4–10

[Jesus said,] "This is a wicked generation; it is asking for a sign. The only sign it will be given is the sign of Jonah. . . . On Judgment day the men of Nineveh will stand up with this generation and condemn it, because when Jonah preached they repented; and there is something greater than Jonah here."

LUKE 11:29, 32

Jonah's prophecy is a witty commentary on the contrast between the mercy of God for all creation on the one hand and the cowardice, narrowness, and harshness of God's chosen people, personified in Jonah, on the other.

God calls on the prophet Jonah to preach to Nineveh, Israel's powerful and cruel pagan neighbor. Jonah decides instead to run away, and he boards a ship heading in the opposite direction. The ship is hit by a storm, and the pagan sailors pray for deliverance. Meanwhile, God's chosen one is asleep in the hold. Eventually Jonah admits to the sailors that his disobedience is the cause of the disaster and tells the sailors that the sea will become calm only if they throw him into it. Frightened of God, the sailors reluctantly cast Jonah overboard. He ends up in the great fish, which conveniently delivers him to Nineveh, many hundreds of miles inland. He preaches, and the Ninevites repent, with even the animals fasting. When God relents and does not destroy the city, Jonah is bitterly disappointed. In the hope that God might revert to his original plan, Jonah sits in the shade of a castor-oil plant on a hillside overlooking the city, awaiting the destruction of the evil empire. He sits there overnight, and when he awakes the next morning the plant has withered. Jonah suffers in the scorching wind and burning sun and begs for death. The prophecy ends with God saying to Jonah, "You are only upset about a castor-oil plant which cost you no labor, which you did not make grow. . . . Am I not to feel sorry for Nineveh, the great city, in which there are more than a hundred and twenty thousand people who cannot tell their right hand from their left, to say nothing of all the animals?" (Jonah 4:10–11).

In the Gospel, Jesus denounces the Jews for looking for signs, assuring them that the only sign they will find is the sign that was given to Jonah.

We are still looking for signs—the dramatic healing, the apparitions, the whirling sun, and so on. The real sign, the miracle, is not in these external happenings but in the inner conversion of mind and heart, as the Ninevites discovered through Jonah's preaching.

Prayer

> *Deliver us, Lord, from triumphalism in all its forms. Whenever we encounter anyone of a different faith or of no faith, help us to tread warily and reverently, for you have been there before us and your living Spirit is in every heart. We ask you this through Jesus Christ, our Lord. Amen.*

Thursday

PETITION

Esther 4:17; Psalm 138; Matthew 7:7–12

[Jesus said to his disciples:] "Ask, and it will be given to you; search, and you will find; knock, and the door will be opened to you. For the one who asks always receives; the one who searches always finds; the one who knocks will always have the door opened. . . . Is there a man among you who would hand his son a stone when he asked for bread? Or would hand him a snake when he asked for a fish? If you, then, who are evil, know how to give your children what is good, how much more will your Father in heaven give good things to those who ask him! So always treat others as you would like them to treat you; that is the meaning of the Law and the Prophets."

MATTHEW 7:7–12

I have sometimes wondered whether the Gospel writers did not slip up on this passage, which should have read, "Ask, and it will not be given to you."

Christians are divided over the need for and the value of petitionary prayer. Some Christians are obsessive petitioners, behaving as though God is an absentminded God who, if not constantly prompted, will forget to notice our needs and those of our friends. Others abandon petitionary prayer altogether because they assume that God already knows our needs. Yet the Gospels are clear—"Ask, and it will be given to you." It is not a misprint. In fact, Jesus recommends that we pester God like the widow who pesters the judge or like the man who wakes up his friend in the middle of the night to ask him for bread: "I tell you, if the man does not get up and give it him for friendship's sake, persistence will be enough to make him get up and give his friend all he wants" (Luke 11:8).

In spite of the clarity of Jesus' statement, petitionary prayer does raise questions, such as "What am I expecting God to do when I pray?" For example, when I pray before a train journey, am I asking God to sharpen up the driver's reflexes or to tighten up any loose bolts that the maintenance engineers may have overlooked? And when I pray for others, am I asking God to suspend nature's laws for the sake of my friends, to protect Fred's liver from the ruinous effects of the alcohol he has consumed? When football season begins, do I pray fervently to God to allow my team to win? Do we expect God to comply with all our prayers, from our everyday requests to our desperate pleadings?

The point of petitionary prayer is not that we receive precisely what we ask for but that we acknowledge and deepen our dependence on God and gradually learn to sift our real needs from our wants by putting our requests into words. When I pray for a safe journey, to win a bet, or for a sick friend, I am praying for the enrichment of my own and other people's lives.

If we reflect on our own lives, we will realize the difficulty we have in distinguishing our wants from our needs. We may feel that we need more money, success, and popularity. But if we receive these things, they may create more problems for us. If we do not receive them but we continue to trust in God, we can begin to understand that our lack of money can teach us to appreciate our need for inner wealth, peace of mind, and inner contentment. Our failure to succeed or earn the approval of others may free us from living to meet other people's expectations and allow us to live in obedience to the deeper promptings of our hearts. It is in those deeper nudgings that we can find the will of God, who desires our good more than we can ever desire it for ourselves.

Prayer

> *God, give us a childlike trust that we live enfolded in your goodness, that in every event and encounter, no matter how dark or disappointing it may be to us, you are there, protecting, welcoming, cherishing, and leading us to you. We ask you this through Jesus Christ, our Lord. Amen.*

Friday

RECONCILIATION

Ezekiel 18:21–28; Psalm 130;
Matthew 5:20–26

*[It is Yahweh who speaks,] "If the wicked man renounces
all the sins he has committed, respects my laws and is
law-abiding and honest, he will certainly live; he will not
die. . . . What! Am I likely to take pleasure in the death of
a wicked man—it is the Lord Yahweh who speaks—and
not prefer to see him renounce his wickedness and live? . . .
When the upright man renounces his integrity to commit
sin and dies because of this, he dies because of the evil that
he himself has committed."*

EZEKIEL 18:21, 23, 26

*[Jesus said,] "If you are bringing your offering to the altar
and there remember that your brother has something
against you, leave your offering there before the altar, go
and be reconciled with your brother first, and then come
back and present your offering."*

MATTHEW 5:23—24

When hitchhiking on one occasion, I was given a lift by an Irish Buddhist who told me that Buddhism attracted him because its system of beliefs does not include a concept of sin. He had found the concept of sin very destructive in his former Catholic life because it filled him with fear and guilt.

Some instruction on sin is itself sinful. Oftentimes it presents us with a God who, "in his infinite mercy," has planted minefields of sin all over our world. Some of these sins wound us, though not fatally, and are called "venial," while others kill us and are called "mortal." God entrusts the secret of the exact location and explosive power of these mines to the clergy, who relay it to the faithful through their teaching, preaching, and writing. The effects of learning this information are deadly, either leading people to reject the whole notion of God, and therefore of sin, or crippling them with fear, anxiety, timidity, and neuroticism.

Sin is not the same thing as wrongdoing or lawbreaking. *Sin* is a religious word that means an offense against the living God, who is love and who is present in all things and all people. God is, in the words of Gerard Manley Hopkins, "World's strand, sway of the sea, Lord of the living and dead."

To sin is to not let God be the God of love, tenderness, and compassion. We must not go to the altar until we have been reconciled with our brother because we cannot be at one with God until we are ready to be at one with those who have offended us. We wish that God had not arranged it so, and we try to solve the problem by convincing ourselves that God must be on our side so that we are justified in continuing our feuds. Religious people can be especially guilty of this. In refusing to be reconciled, we harm not only our enemies but also ourselves because we cut ourselves off from God's life and love. God does not punish us; we inflict punishment on ourselves. "What! Am I likely to take pleasure in the death of a wicked man?" (Ezekiel 18:23).

To sin is to not let God be God, to forget his goodness. We may never do wrong or break a law, but we still sin because the aim of our life is to protect our own respectability or rectitude, which we pursue without love.

Prayer

> *Enlighten our minds and hearts, Lord, so that in recognizing you in our own lives and in the life of the world we may detect, abhor, and oppose all attitudes and actions that are destructive of your love within and around us. We ask you this through Jesus Christ, our Lord. Amen.*

Saturday

ON BEING PERFECT

Deuteronomy 26:16–19; Psalm 119;
Matthew 5:43–48

And Yahweh has today made this declaration about you:
that you will be his very own people as he promised you, but
only if you keep all his commandments . . . and you will be
a people consecrated to Yahweh, as he promised.

DEUTERONOMY 26:18–19

[Jesus said to his disciples,] "You have learned how it was
said: You must love your neighbor and hate your enemy.
But I say this to you: love your enemies and pray for those
who persecute you; in this way you will be sons of your Father
in heaven, for he causes his sun to rise on bad men as well
as good, and his rain to fall on honest and dishonest men
alike. . . . You must therefore be perfect just as your heavenly
Father is perfect."

MATTHEW 5:43–45, 48

It is difficult enough to keep loving those who love us or
even to love our friendly neighbors, but Jesus says, "Love

your enemies," those who have damaged us and may still wish us harm. He tells us to do this because God acts in this way, and "you will be his very own people as he promised you, but only if you keep all his commandments."

"Be perfect just as your heavenly Father is perfect" is a phrase often repeated out of context and a source of anxiety for many Christians, who interpret *perfect* as meaning "in complete conformity to a system of set rules and ritual observances." I knew a headmaster who preached to his pupils on this phrase and then applied it to the students' observance of all the school's rules, which were many and included a permitted length of hair. It is possible to be perfect in this sense, so utterly dedicated to the system or rule book that we have no time or energy left to love even those who are nearest to us, never mind our enemies. In fact, the greater our allegiance to a system and to perfection in this sense, the more people we will find to dislike because they do not conform to our system. We often hear someone described as a "most dedicated" priest/vicar/deacon/parishioner. To what are they dedicated? is the question. Jesus spoke of the dedication of the Pharisees, "who travel over land and sea to make a single proselyte," and then added that "when [they] have him [they] make him twice as fit for hell as [they] are." He goes on to describe them as a "brood of vipers" and "whitewashed tombs." The test of true dedication is how the dedicated person reacts to those who criticize, disagree with, or oppose his or her ideas and actions. A truly dedicated person will always be tolerant of others and will listen carefully to opponents, think well of them, and treat them as friends.

Rules of life, religious observances, and rituals are all useful and necessary, but if they are not leading us to a greater love of God, our neighbor, and our enemies, then they are of little avail, no matter how many hours we pray or how long we fast. Loving our enemies includes accepting and loving ourselves, especially our dark side and those parts of ourselves that are far from perfect and of which we are ashamed. We cannot achieve this by an act of will but by acknowledging these aspects of ourselves and showing them to God. We must then trust that he accepts us as we are, is full of compassion, and is saying to us "Though your sins are like scarlet, they shall be as white as snow" (Isaiah 1:18).

Prayer

> *Deliver us, Lord, from every form of self-righteousness and from glorying in our own goodness. Give us the eyes to see and the courage to face our own sinfulness, so that by acknowledging it and trusting that you love us in our sinfulness we may show that same compassion even to our enemies. We ask you this through Jesus Christ, our Lord. Amen.*

Sunday

THE TRANSFIGURATION

Genesis 12:1–4; Matthew 17:1–9

*Yahweh said to Abram, "Leave your country, your family
and your father's house, for the land I will show you. I will
make you a great nation."*

GENESIS 12:1—2

*Jesus took with him Peter and James and his brother John
and led them up a high mountain. . . . There in their
presence he was transfigured: his face shone like the sun and
his clothes became as white as the light. Suddenly Moses and
Elijah appeared to them. . . . Then Peter spoke to Jesus.
"Lord," he said, "it is wonderful for us to be here; if you wish,
I will make three tents here, one for you, one for Moses and
one for Elijah." He was still speaking when suddenly a bright
cloud covered them with shadow, and from the cloud there
came a voice which said, "This is my Son, the Beloved; he
enjoys my favor. Listen to him." When they heard this, the
disciples fell on their faces, overcome with fear. But Jesus came
up and touched them. "Stand up," he said, "do not be
afraid." And when they raised their eyes they saw no one
but only Jesus.*

MATTHEW 17:1—8

We read the Scriptures in order to find the God of Abraham and of Jesus in our own lives. God did not just give Abram orders from on high; he entered into a covenant with Abram. At that time, nomadic peoples entered into covenants with one another for their mutual protection, promising that in the future "my enemies will be your enemies, my friends will be your friends." The contracting parties then dismembered an animal, laid the dismembered parts on the ground, and walked between the parts and declared, "If I am untrue to this covenant, may the same happen to me as has happened to this animal." In Genesis 15, God tells Abram to take animals, cut them in half, lay them on the ground, and leave a space between the halves. At night a firebrand appears between the halves. "That day Yahweh made a Covenant with Abram" (Genesis 15:18).

In Christian understanding, Jesus is the fulfillment of this covenant because in him God has entered into the closest possible covenant with us. Jesus said, "The Father and I are one" (John 10:30), but he also said, "in so far as you did this to one of the least of these brothers of mine, you did it to me" (Matthew 25:40). God and human beings are inseparably bonded. "The life you have," Paul said, "is hidden with Christ in God" (Colossians 3:3). Our journey's destination is God, and we move toward him as we move toward one another in truth, justice, and love. On the journey we meet with opposition not only from outside but most of all from within ourselves, for the paths of untruth, injustice, and violence offer us advancement, security, acclaim, and popularity, while the paths of truth, justice, and love can threaten our wealth, position, and even our lives, as we saw when Jesus was threatened. Just before the Transfiguration Jesus warns, "If anyone wants to be a follower of mine, let him renounce himself and take up his cross every day and follow me" (Luke 9:23).

The Transfiguration is a momentary revelation of the reality of Jesus, the fulfillment of the Law and the Prophets, Emmanuel, God with us. The human experience of the holiness of God has been described as *tremendum et fascinans*, that is, it both attracts and frightens. Peter is attracted to God's holiness and wants the experience to be permanent, but he is also frightened and falls to the ground. Jesus says, "Do not be afraid," and the disciples see "only Jesus."

We should pray on this passage imaginatively, begging God to give us a glimpse of the glory in which we are living. We are caught up in a drama in which the whole of creation is involved, and it is much more complex than we can ever imagine. "From the beginning till now the entire creation, as we know, has been groaning in one great act of giving birth" (Romans 8:22). Our minds form ideas and images of God as being outside and beyond us, but God is also within us, enveloping us, cherishing and delighting in us. This is the reality. It is right that we should ask for a glimpse of this glory so that afterward we may know that our present state of perception is distorted, that "we are seeing a dim reflection in a mirror" (1 Corinthians 13:12). During the Transfiguration, the disciples glimpsed the reality; afterward, when they saw "only Jesus," the full reality was again hidden from them. Pray for an inner knowledge, which is deeper than a sensible feeling or any neatly formulated thought, that our life really is "hidden with Christ in God."

Prayer

Lord, give us a glimpse of the reality in which we are now living, enfolded in your goodness, and give us hope in the glory you have promised us. We ask you this through Jesus Christ, our Lord. Amen.

Monday

ON BEING COMPASSIONATE

Daniel 9:4–10; Psalm 79; Luke 6:36–38

To the Lord our God mercy and pardon belong, because we have betrayed him, and have not listened to the voice of Yahweh our God nor followed the laws he has given us.

DANIEL 9:9–10

[Jesus said to his disciples:] "Be compassionate as your Father is compassionate. Do not judge, and you will not be judged yourselves; do not condemn, and you will not be condemned yourselves; grant pardon, and you will be pardoned. Give, and there will be gifts for you: a full measure, pressed down, shaken together, and running over, will be poured into your lap; because the amount you measure out is the amount you will be given back."

LUKE 6:36–38

One of the symptoms of our split spirituality, which we discussed in the first chapter, is the way in which we regard penance. Instead of seeing penance as an attitude of mind that should affect every aspect of life—secular as well as sacred, public as well as private—we see it as a solitary action to be performed at particular times, such as Lent, and one that requires giving up certain pleasures or enduring some hardship.

The prophets demanded repentance from Israel, and this passage from Daniel is a typical expression of Jewish national repentance. It is rare for any church to repent publicly of its sins except in the most general terms. It is rare too for any public institution, political party, or nation to repent publicly of its past crimes. An admission of guilt is considered a weakness, so the tendency is to justify the wrongdoing and deny the guilt. When there is no confession of guilt, there can be no healing or real reconciliation. Peace imposed through power can suppress external violence for a time, but violence breeds violence, and sooner or later it will erupt, more destructive than before.

Penance means a change of mind and heart. Luke sums this up by saying, "Be compassionate, as your Father is compassionate," and then elaborating on his meaning. One of the best commentaries I have ever read on this passage is by Carl Rogers, a counselor who did not profess to be a Christian. He advocated listening "with unconditional positive regard," a clumsy but important phrase that means listening without judging or condemning others, neither approving nor disapproving, whatever their views or behavior, but always thinking well of them as persons. Rogers also recommended employing "empathy," the ability to enter into the mind and heart of others, to walk in their shoes for a while. When people listen to us in this way, we are much more likely to discover for ourselves what is creative and what is destructive in our lives. This is the knowledge that effects change, a process beautifully summed up in the book of Wisdom: "Overlook men's sins so that they can repent" (Wisdom 11:24).

We are reluctant to be compassionate beyond a certain level because compassion is risky and may demand change. Bishop Helder Camara said, "When I give a starving man food, they call me a saint: when I ask why he is starving, they call me a communist." Listening to other people's ideas and beliefs can lead us to question our own, which can be very threatening to us. It is much more comfortable in the short term to avoid compassion, seal ourselves off from disturbing influences, and declare any threatening ideas or attitudes to be wrong while defending ourselves against them. In this way we build a divided world in which a fraction of the money spent on destructive weaponry could feed the millions doomed to starvation and house the homeless poor.

The call to repentance, to compassion, is not just a call intended for devout Christians; it is a call intended for the whole human race and one that concerns the survival of us all. If we can learn to listen to that call as individuals, groups, and nations, then the gifts we will receive will be "pressed down and flowing over."

Prayer

> *Lord, we thank you for the gift of hearing. Help us to use this gift so that as individuals, groups, and nations, we may learn to listen without judging or condemning and to pardon and forgive as you pardon and forgive us. We ask you this through Jesus Christ, our Lord. Amen.*

Tuesday

ONLY ONE TEACHER

Isaiah 1:10, 16–20; Psalm 50;
Matthew 23:1–12

WEEK THREE

Addressing the people and his disciples Jesus said, "The scribes and the Pharisees occupy the chair of Moses. You must therefore do what they tell you and listen to what they say; but do not be guided by what they do: since they do not practice what they preach. . . . Everything they do is done to attract attention . . . being greeted obsequiously in the market squares and having people call them Rabbi. You, however, must not allow yourselves to be called Rabbi, since you have only one Master, and you are all brothers. You must call no one on earth your father, since you have only one Father, and he is in heaven. Nor must you allow yourselves to be called teachers, for you have only one Teacher, the Christ. The greatest among you must be your servant. Anyone who exalts himself will be humbled, and anyone who humbles himself will be exalted."

MATTHEW 23:1–3, 5, 7–12

It is astonishing that this clear preaching of Jesus has been so successfully ignored in the history of the church. Those in authority still wear distinctive dress, have special places of honor in church and at banquets, and are addressed with much more obsequious titles than "Rabbi" or "teacher," which sound very modest compared with some of our titles, such as Your Holiness, Your Excellency, Your Eminence, Your Grace, Your Lordship, and Your Reverence.

Jesus proposes a new kind of society in which the greatest become the least and the leaders become the servants, a proposal that would revolutionize church and state and is, therefore, sedulously avoided by both.

How realistic is this teaching? Can we do without rabbis and teachers, parent-child relationships, and experts? Inevitably, some people are going to be more knowledgeable, capable, and intelligent than others, and we will all be in need of one another's special abilities. Jesus is not denying this truth, but he is warning the more knowledgeable against exercising a tyranny of knowledge over those whom they teach, and he is also warning students against becoming subservient to those who teach them. This warning is even more necessary in our bureaucratic, technological age than it was in Jesus' time, for the multiplying scientific disciplines and the growth in specialization can lead us to leave everything to the experts. The experts are delighted that this should be so, and we become increasingly powerless and surrender our most precious gift, our freedom. In every profession, including theology and spirituality, professionals exhibit an elitist separatism that shows itself in many ways, such as in the use of technical language, which mystifies the uninitiated and renders him or her more helpless. Reflect on your own dealings with doctors, lawyers, educators, psychologists, members of the clergy, and theologians.

One of the most tragic aspects of life in our inner cities is not the shortage of money and food, although that is bad enough, but the inner demoralization of people caught in the poverty trap. They are made to feel that there is nothing they can do to effect change, that they have no worth, no say, and nothing to contribute. People caught in homelessness or in the poverty trap of the inner city need others to listen to them, to encourage them to express themselves in their own ways, and to give them some say in the ordering of their lives. But it is not only the economically poor who need this encouragement to rely on their own judgment, to have confidence in themselves, and to drink from their own wells. The need is widespread and especially present in the church and in all religious education. The primary functions of those in authority in the church are to listen to people, to encourage them to express their own thoughts, needs, and aspirations, and to build up each person's self-confidence. A clerically dominated church is a contradiction of Jesus' clear teaching and is in fact destructive of faith. Personal faith in God is impossible unless believers also have faith in their own judgment. The Spirit dwells within us, and authority figures in the church should enable people to become more aware and responsive to the Spirit of God within them.

Prayer

> *God, you have sent the Holy Spirit, who lived in Jesus and raised him from the dead, into our hearts. Deepen our faith in the presence of your Spirit within us so that we can recognize you, our teacher, and obey your promptings, for our own good and the good of all your people. We ask you this through Jesus Christ, our Lord. Amen.*

Wednesday

SERVICE

Jeremiah 18:18–20; Psalm 31;
Matthew 20:17–28

[Jesus said,] "Now we are going up to Jerusalem, and the Son of Man is about to be handed over to the chief priests and scribes. They will condemn him to death and will hand him over to the pagans to be mocked and scourged and crucified; and on the third day he will rise again." . . .

She [the mother of Zebedee's sons] said to him, "Promise that these two sons of mine may sit one at your right hand and the other at your left in your kingdom. . . ." When the other ten heard this they were indignant with the two brothers. But Jesus called them to him and said, "You know that among the pagans the rulers lord it over them, and their great men make their authority felt. This is not to happen among you. No; anyone who wants to be great among you must be your servant, and anyone who wants to be first among you must be your slave, just as the Son of Man came not to be served but to serve, and to give his life as a ransom for many."

MATTHEW 20:18–19, 21, 24–28

We are so familiar with the word *Christian* that we forget its meaning. The German word for "Christian" is *Ein Christ*, a Christ. To be a Christian is not just to be an admirer, imitator, or follower of Christ but to live so that, as Paul says, "I live now not with my own life but with the life of Christ who lives in me" (Galatians 2:20). In this book we are looking at our lives in the light of this truth so that we can see more clearly what is in fact life giving and what is life destroying. Today's Gospel passage raises questions for all of us about the directions our lives are taking.

The mother of the two apostles wants the best for her sons just as the two brothers and the other ten apostles want the best for themselves. Jesus then speaks to them all about their desire for power, status, and influence.

It is natural, good, and healthy to desire greatness and want to excel. Jesus does not deny this, but he turns our value systems upside down by saying that true greatness and true excellence consist not in people who exercise power and control over others but in those who serve the needs of others and are content to be slaves. "His state was divine, yet he did not cling to his equality with God but emptied himself to assume the condition of a slave" (Philippians 2:6–7).

In the Gospels, Jesus gives no detailed instruction about how his church should be organized, but he is very clear on how authority should be exercised within it. We have followed Jesus' instructions more in the letter than in the spirit. We have applied his literal meaning to some ecclesiastical titles and religious terms, such as the pope's title, "servant of servants," the words *ministry* and *minister* from the Latin word *ministrare*, which means "to serve," and the title "deacon," which means "a menial." But if we were to follow the spirit of Jesus' instructions, it would effect a revolution in the community of the church and in society. A promotion to a position of authority would bring about diminished status, a drop in salary, less power to control, and greater accessibility. The first task of those in authority would be to listen to the needs of those they serve.

We can escape the demands of this teaching by believing it applies only to church officials. But we are all "Christs" and are all called to serve rather than be served. When we review our day, it is good to examine the moods we experienced and ask ourselves the question "Are these moods arising from my desire to serve or from my desire to be served?" This is a painful question for us to ask ourselves because it reveals the split within our own spirituality: how easily our minds assent to Jesus' ideal of service, while our hearts are in fact choosing the opposite. Do not be disheartened if you are aware of this split in yourself, but acknowledge it before God. Pray from the sheepdog part of yourself that Christ's Spirit will lead you to take more delight in serving, listening to, and letting others be free than in controlling or being served by others.

Prayer

> *Lord, you did not cling to your equality with God, but emptied yourself to assume the condition of a slave. Root out from our hearts all desire for power and influence over others and plant in its place a love and delight in serving you by listening and responding to the needs of others. We ask you this through Jesus Christ, our Lord. Amen.*

Thursday

RICHES AND POVERTY

Jeremiah 17:5–10; Psalm 1;
Luke 16:19–31

[Yahweh says this,] "The heart is more devious than any
other thing, perverse too: who can pierce its secrets?"

JEREMIAH 17:9

[Jesus said,] "There was a rich man who used to dress in
purple and fine linen and feast magnificently every day.
And at his gate there lay a poor man called Lazarus, cov-
ered with sores, who longed to fill himself with the scraps
that fell from the rich man's table. . . . Now the poor man
died. . . . The rich man also died.
*   "In his torment in Hades [Dives] . . . cried out, 'Father*
Abraham, pity me and send Lazarus to dip the tip of his
finger in water and cool my tongue, for I am in agony in
these flames.'"

LUKE 16:19—24

Abraham says that no one can cross the gulf between Dives
and Lazarus. When Dives asks Abraham to send Lazarus to

warn Dives's brothers of the torment they will experience if they come to Hades, Abraham replies that if they will not listen to Moses and the prophets, they will not be convinced even if someone should rise from the dead.

Dives represents the wealthy class, Lazarus the poor. Dives is not portrayed as a malicious persecutor who oppresses or exploits Lazarus; Dives simply does not notice Lazarus, and that is the most disturbing element of the parable.

A British cabinet minister stated recently that poverty no longer existed in Britain. His statement came at a time when the rich were becoming richer, the poor were becoming poorer, many were without enough to eat, and homelessness was increasing. The government, meanwhile, through cuts in social services, was putting extra burdens on those least able to bear them.

Our situation is mild compared with that of Third World countries, where a billion people are malnourished and thousands die daily of starvation, not because food is lacking but because it is unjustly distributed.

In developed countries, explanations for why poverty exists exonerate the wealthy from any blame and from any obligation to redress the situation. Third World poverty is attributed to the backwardness of its peoples and the corruptness of its governments and officials, while poverty in the United States is attributed to the fecklessness of the poor, who spend their money on alcohol and tobacco instead of on wholesome food. In the face of all this poverty, the wealthy have a simple answer: "Create more wealth." Their belief is that more wealth will result in a trickle-down effect from which the poor will eventually benefit. But this theory is not verified by statistics or past experience. "The heart is more devious than any other thing" (Jeremiah 17:9). Meanwhile, the cost of one Trident submarine to defend a wealthy nation is equivalent to the total educational budget of twenty-three developing countries.

Our spirituality is so split that most Christians believe that world hunger, homelessness, the arms trade, and war itself are political, not religious, issues and are therefore unsuitable topics for the pulpit. Such a split spirituality is attractive to the wealthy, just as it was attractive to Dives and enabled him to dine sumptuously every day without even noticing Lazarus.

The problems of world injustice are massive, complex, and apparently intractable. As individuals, what can we do? First, we must acknowledge that these are religious issues. To ignore them is to ignore God and live a practical atheism. Second, we must not only inform our parishes and ourselves about poverty in our own countries and abroad but also befriend some of its victims.

Prayer

> *God, create a clean and compassionate heart within us. Deliver us from all deviousness, so that we can face the plight of the poor at home and abroad, and in doing so, understand their plight, and in understanding, work to put right the structures and attitudes that keep Dives feasting while Lazarus starves. We ask you this through Jesus Christ, our Lord. Amen.*

Friday

PROVIDENCE

Genesis 37:3–28; Psalm 105;
Matthew 21:33–46

[His brothers] saw him in the distance, and before he
reached them they made a plot among themselves to put
him to death. "Here comes the man of dreams," they said
to one another. "Come on, let us kill him and throw him
into some well; we can say that a wild beast devoured him.
Then we shall see what becomes of his dreams."

GENESIS 37:18—20

Jesus tells the chief priests and elders the parable of the
landowner who built a vineyard and then sent his servants
to collect the produce from the tenants. The tenants kill
the servants and then kill the second round of servants the
landowner sends. When the landowner sends his son the
tenants say, "This is the heir. Come on, let us kill him and
take over his inheritance." After Jesus tells the parable, he
says to the scribes and chief priests, "I tell you, then, that
the kingdom of God will be taken from you and given to
a people who will produce its fruit" (Matthew 21:43).

WEEK THREE

The Gospel accounts of Jesus' passion and death include the constant refrain "as Scripture ordained" or "now all this happened to fulfill the prophecies in Scripture," strange phrases that, if taken literally, seem to nullify our freedom of will. If we have no human freedom, we have no guilt, no sin, and no need of redemption or forgiveness.

The opening verse of Genesis includes the statement "There was darkness over the deep, and God's Spirit hovered over the water." This is an eternal truth, for God's Spirit is always hovering over our individual and corporate chaos and bringing life and order out of it, a theme that runs throughout the whole Bible story. We are free and can freely reject God, but God is always greater than we are and can bring good out of our evil. On Holy Saturday the church sings, in the ancient hymn called the Exsultet, "O happy sin of Adam, which brought us such a redeemer!" When Joseph becomes chief steward in Egypt and his hungry brothers come looking for food, Joseph eventually reveals himself to them and says, "Do not grieve, do not reproach yourselves for having sold me here, since God sent me before you to preserve your lives" (Genesis 45:5).

In John's account of the Passion, after the human beings have done their worst and have pierced the side of Christ with a lance, he says, "There came out blood and water," which John sees as the blood and water in which we are redeemed. Repeating the phrase "as Scripture ordained" is perhaps a way of reminding us that no human action, no matter how evil, can ever suppress the creative power of God's love.

We need to ponder the truth of this in our own lives. We have damaged others and ourselves just as others, including our parents and teachers, have, usually unintentionally, damaged us. It is sometimes only in later life that we become aware of this deep-seated damage and the lifelong affliction it has caused. We can spend the rest of our lives regretting the damage we have done and resenting the damage done to us by others. Instead, we have to acknowledge this damage, hand it over to God, and let his Spirit hover over it and transform it. Our faith teaches us that no situation, no individual, no group is ever hopeless.

In the parable, Jesus warns the Jewish authorities, the chief priests and elders, that that the kingdom of God will be taken from them and given to a people who will produce its fruit. The parable is included in the Gospels as a warning to the church, for the church too can lose sight of its vocation, become more concerned with its maintenance than its mission, and fail to recognize God's work in the signs of the times. In our own era, the clearest messages and most effective action for world peace have not come from Western leaders who claimed to be Christian. In championing the oppressed and defending human rights, unbelievers have often been more compassionate than believers.

Prayer

> God, in the beginning, now, and forever, your life-giving Spirit hovers over our chaos, bringing order out of disorder, light out of darkness, life from death. Deepen our faith in your unbounded goodness, so that in finding hope in our own brokenness we can encourage the afflicted to find hope when everything seems hopeless and support them in their search. We ask you this through Jesus Christ, our Lord. Amen.

Saturday

GOD WELCOMES SINNERS

Micah 7:14–20; Psalm 103; Luke 15:1–32

WEEK THREE

Once more have pity on us, tread down our faults, to the bottom of the sea throw all our sins.

MICAH 7:19

"Here am I dying of hunger! I will leave this place and go to my father and say: Father, I have sinned against heaven and against you; I no longer deserve to be called your son. . . . " While he was still a long way off, his father saw him and was moved with pity. He ran to the boy, clasped him in his arms and kissed him tenderly. . . . "Quick! Bring out the best robe and put it on him; put a ring on his finger and sandals on his feet. Bring the calf we have been fattening, and kill it; we are going to have a feast, a celebration, because this son of mine was dead and has come back to life; he was lost and is found." . . .

[The elder son] was angry then and refused to go in. . . . "All these years I have slaved for you and never once disobeyed your orders, yet you never offered me so much as a kid for me to celebrate with my friends. But, for this son of

yours, when he comes back after swallowing up your prop-
erty—he and his women—you kill the calf we had been
fattening." The father said, "My son, you are with me
always and all I have is yours. But it was only right we
should celebrate and rejoice, because your brother here was
dead and has come to life; he was lost and is found."

LUKE 15:17—20, 22—24, 28—32

When the Pharisees and scribes complain that Jesus "welcomes sinners and eats with them," Jesus replies with
three parables: the lost drachma, the lost sheep, and what
is usually called the parable of the prodigal son. This final
parable is really the story of two sons, both lost, but in
very different ways.

Because it is so familiar, the parable can bounce off the
surface of our minds, so it is important to contemplate it
imaginatively—seeing the Pharisees complaining to Jesus
and then, as Jesus tells the story, imagining that it is now
happening. Prayed in this way, the story can unearth
material from deep layers of our consciousness of which
we were once unaware.

With our lips and our heads we can say that God is a
God of mercy and compassion, but at a deeper level of
consciousness we may think of him as God the judge,
whose primary interest is in our sins and their appropriate
punishment. If such is our image, then we will measure
closeness to God as being in direct proportion to sinless-
ness, and estrangement from God in proportion to offenses
committed. Any contrary teaching will seem heretical, and
our sympathy will be for the elder son in the story.

Jesus presents a totally different picture of God. This
scandalized the Pharisees, who then felt justified in getting rid of Jesus, the blasphemer. The parable questions

our image of God: is it Jesus' image or that of the Pharisees?

God welcomes the prodigal, you and me, not because of our merits or achievements but simply because we are his. God is represented as the father waiting for the child as though he had no other interest, recognizing his son even when he is still a long way off, rushing out to meet him, and apparently not hearing his confession of guilt. In prayer, meet God and feel him welcome you. What response do you want to make?

The elder brother represents the Pharisee in us, the God-the-judge part of us that resents God's generosity toward those who do not live up to our standards of respectability and correctness. The Pharisee relishes his moral superiority. It is this attitude that has turned so many people away from the church—such as single parents, men and women who are divorced, alcoholics, and AIDS sufferers—the very people whom God the shepherd pursues, rejoicing in them when they are found.

Prayer

> *Lord, lover of all your creation, cleanse our minds and hearts of all false images of you. Show us your love of us so that we may reflect your welcome to everyone we encounter. We ask you this through Jesus Christ, our Lord. Amen.*

Sunday

THE WELL WITHIN

Exodus 17:3–7; Romans 5:1–8;
John 4:5–42

> *The people complained against Moses. "Why did you bring*
> *us out of Egypt?" they said. "Was it so that I should die of*
> *thirst, my children too, and my cattle?" Moses appealed to*
> *Yahweh. "How am I to deal with this people?" he said. "A*
> *little more and they will stone me!" Yahweh said to Moses,*
> *. . . "You must strike the rock, and water will flow from it*
> *for the people to drink."*

EXODUS 17:3—6

Today's Gospel, which relates Jesus' encounter with the
Samaritan woman, is quite long, so I shall give a brief
commentary and a few quotations.

I heard a Sikh give an address at the funeral of Stella
Reekie, a Church of Scotland deaconess. He said that
Stella was like water, "for she gave us life, cleansed and
refreshed us. But she was also like water because she
assumed the shape of whoever she was with, so that to
me, Stella was a Sikh, to my Muslim friends a Muslim, to

Jews she was Jewish." It was a wonderful tribute; the Sikh recognized a life-giving quality in Stella and so compared her to water, a scriptural image for the life of God.

It is remarkable that the famous discourse on God as living water should be given to a Samaritan woman at Jacob's well because no self-respecting Jew would normally have talked with a Samaritan, who was considered worse than a pagan and therefore to be avoided and despised. That is why the woman replies to Jesus' request for a drink with "What? You are a Jew and you ask me, a Samaritan, for a drink?"

Jesus says to her, "If you only knew what God is offering and who it is that is saying to you: Give me a drink, you would have been the one to ask, and he would have given you living water." The woman answers, "You have no bucket, sir, and the well is deep," discounting, with this piece of common sense, Jesus' revelation of himself as the giver of eternal life. Like the woman at the well, we are constantly laying down criteria to which God must match up if he is going to have any chance of being accepted by us. It was the same in Jesus' own lifetime: People would say, "Is he not a carpenter's son? Prophets do not come out of Galilee." We lay down conditions that must be fulfilled before we will pay serious attention. If the reality with which we are presented does not fit into our mental filing system, then the reality is denied or ignored. A headmaster, after being informed late one evening by a staff member with a drinking problem that the school was on fire, said, "You're drunk," and a wing of the school burned down. It is useful to make out a list of our "you have no bucket" phrases and then pray to be delivered from every form of prejudice, bigotry, snobbishness, and attachment, including religious attachment, that blinds us to the gifts God is offering us in the truth of things.

It is to this openness to truth that Jesus invites the woman: "Believe me, woman, the hour is coming when you will worship the Father neither on this mountain nor in Jerusalem. . . . The hour will come—in fact it is here already—when true worshipers will worship the Father in spirit and truth: that is the kind of worshiper the Father wants. God is spirit, and those who worship must worship in spirit and truth" (John 4:21, 23–24).

We cannot find God simply by worshiping in a particular place, or in a particular church, or with a particular form of service. The place, the church, and the form of service are important, but only as a means to help us worship in spirit and in truth. When we forget this, it leads to divisions between and within Christian churches. When we meet together across denominations to pray silently in spirit and in truth, and when we meet to serve Christ together by working for our local and wider communities, then we will come to know the spring within us that is welling up to eternal life.

Prayer

> *Lord, deliver us from searching for our ultimate security in any created thing, in any theory, system, or organization, sacred or secular. Show yourself to us, our light, our refuge, our salvation, so that we may recognize you in all things and worship you always in spirit and in truth. We ask you this through Jesus Christ, our Lord. Amen.*

Monday

GOD OF ALL NATIONS

2 Kings 5:1–15; Psalms 42, 43;
Luke 4:24–30

So he [Naaman, the Syrian army commander] went down
and immersed himself seven times in the Jordan, as Elisha
had told him to do. And his flesh became clean once more like
the flesh of a little child. Returning to Elisha with his whole
escort, he went in and stood before him. "Now I know," he
said, "that there is no God in all the earth except in Israel."

2 KINGS 5:14—15

[Jesus came to Nazareth and spoke to the people in the syna-
gogue:] "I tell you solemnly, no prophet is ever accepted in his
own country. . . . In the prophet Elisha's time there were
many lepers in Israel, but none of these was cured, except the
Syrian, Naaman." When they heard this everyone in the
synagogue was enraged. They sprang to their feet and hustled
him out of the town; and they took him up to the brow of the
hill their town was built on, intending to throw him down
the cliff, but he slipped through the crowd and walked away.

LUKE 4:24, 27—30

After Jesus' forty days in the desert, Luke writes, "Jesus, with the power of the Spirit in him, returned to Galilee." Jesus then traveled to the synagogue at Nazareth, where at first the congregation approved of him and "were astonished by the gracious words that came from his lips." Nonetheless, they reserved judgment as to his authority ("This is Joseph's son, surely?") and when Jesus began to speak of God's healing of the pagan rather than the Jew, they were enraged, and things went from bad to worse. The sudden change in the congregation's mood from acclaim to murderous rejection seems extraordinary until we reflect a little and realize that we still react in much the same way.

The Old Testament makes it clear that the Israelites were chosen to be God's people, not simply for their own sake but "as a light to the Gentiles," as a sign of God's love for all creation. The people's election was not just a privilege to be enjoyed but a cosmic responsibility to be fulfilled. Yet the Jews often forgot this truth and delighted in their own sense of being the elect. This delight was enhanced by the thought that everyone else was damned, which resulted in the kind of narrowness that is attacked in the prophecy of Jonah.

That same narrow attitude lives on and flourishes in Christianity. Until recently, most Christian denominations justified their separateness by claiming that salvation could be found only in their bodies, so that any step toward another denomination was a step away from God. It would be nice to think that we have left such narrowness behind, but unfortunately we have not. Priests and ministers who practice ecumenism may no longer be hurled over cliffs, but if they try to live according to the ecumenism of Jesus, who came to draw all people to himself, they will soon meet with disapproval. For example, a minister had to leave his parish in Northern Ireland because he had exchanged greetings at Christmas with his Roman Catholic colleague.

The disapproval of ecumenism is usually more subtle, dressed up in the language of orthodoxy. We continue to have our separate churches (we must be loyal to our own traditions), separate training of pastors (because, after all, the needs of our respective people are different), and separate schools (because it is right to ensure that our children will receive a solid grounding in faith). Preaching still tends to warn against dangers rather than invite and encourage people to read the signs of the times and recognize God at work in the most unlikely places. If the clergy, for example, spent more energy in pastorally helping Christians who have married across denominations and less in creating difficulties in such marriages, more energy in promoting Christian unity and less in trying to uphold regulations prohibiting intercommunion, we would all benefit. We would recognize Christ bringing good news to the poor and proclaiming liberty to captives, not in some distant place but in our own minds and hearts and homes.

Prayer

> *O God, free us from all false and distorted images of you, which prevent us from recognizing, learning from, and cooperating with you in your saving action in all peoples. We ask you this through Jesus Christ, our Lord. Amen.*

Tuesday

FORGIVENESS

Daniel 3:25–43; Psalm 25;
Matthew 18:21–35

May the contrite soul, the humbled spirit be as acceptable to
you as holocausts of rams and bullocks.

DANIEL 3:39—40

Peter went up to [Jesus] and said, "Lord, how often must
I forgive my brother if he wrongs me? As often as seven
times?" Jesus answered, "Not seven, I tell you, but seventy-
seven times."

MATTHEW 18:21—22

In the Gospel, Jesus goes on to tell a parable about forgiveness. The parable is about a king who, taking pity
on his debtor, forgives him a debt of ten thousand talents,
almost seven million dollars in our terms. But this debtor,
upon meeting someone who owes him one hundred
denarii, the equivalent of a few dollars, has his debtor
thrown into prison until he pays the tiny sum. When the
king learns of this, he says to his debtor, "You wicked

servant. I canceled all that debt of yours when you appealed to me. Were you not bound, then, to have pity on your fellow servant just as I had pity on you?" And in his anger the king handed his debtor over to the torturers. Jesus ends the parable by saying, "And that is how my heavenly Father will deal with you unless you each forgive your brother from your heart."

"Seventy times seven" is not to be taken literally; it simply means that we must always be ready to forgive. The importance of practicing this gentlest of virtues is expressed in the threatening parable.

In the parable, the king's anger is over the unjust debtor's failure to appreciate what has been done for him. If we are to learn forgiveness, we must first appreciate how much we have been forgiven. For many this is not easy because our religious upbringing can leave us much more conscious of our wrongdoing and guilt than of God's generosity and forgiveness, more aware of our badness than of God's goodness. The more incapable we are of forgiving ourselves, the more condemnatory we are likely to be of others. A useful exercise for those who find self-forgiveness difficult is to imagine Jesus on the cross, suspended over the world, as in the Salvador Dali picture. Tell him, "Lord, I believe that you have reconciled all things by your death on the cross, but do realize, dear Lord, that you have met your match in me."

It is easy to say that God forgives and that therefore we must forgive one another, but it is difficult to put these words to action when we do someone serious harm or are seriously harmed. It is important to acknowledge our difficulty in forgiving others and in believing in the possibility of our own forgiveness, for this difficulty is our meeting place with God. We prefer to avoid it, and we do so by ignoring our own guilt by blaming others and nursing our resentment at the damage done to us. To forgive is divine. The first step for us is to acknowledge our own inability to forgive and to beg God to take over and forgive within us.

True forgiveness does not require pretense. If you have done a serious wrong or have been seriously wronged, then replay the incident in your imagination, and in your imagination express your feelings and thoughts as freely as you can. You may want to take out your frustrations on a pillow, which can represent your offender. Then pause and let your offender speak, giving his or her reasons for hurting you. Now bring Jesus into the scene and listen to what he has to say to each of you.

We can feel forgiven for an offense or able to forgive a particular wrong on one occasion, and then later, when something happens, our guilt or our inability to forgive returns as strongly as ever. Do not be surprised if this should happen, nor let it make you doubt your previous sincerity. We can sincerely forgive and realize we are forgiven at one level of consciousness, but circumstances can reveal to us deeper and yet unredeemed layers within us. How many of these layers are there? As many as seven? "Not seven, I tell you, but seventy times seven!" The inner journey is a journey through these layers, and as we move into deeper layers, the veil hiding God from us grows thinner.

Prayer

> *Come, Holy Spirit, and give my heart's dry roots your nurturing rain. Save me from the unbelief of lingering*

guilt, from harboring grudges and nursing resentments. Open my eyes to the limitlessness of your goodness when, on the cross, you absorbed the violence of our sinfulness and gave us life in return. May your forgiving Spirit live in us now and always. We ask you this through Jesus Christ, our Lord. Amen.

Wednesday

JESUS, THE LAW, AND THE PROPHETS

Deuteronomy 4:1–9; Psalm 147;
Matthew 5:17–19

[Moses said to the people,] "Take notice of the laws and
customs that I teach you today, and observe them, that you
may have life. . . . When they [other peoples] come to know
of all these laws they will exclaim, 'No other people is as wise
and prudent as this great nation.'"

DEUTERONOMY 4:1, 6

[Jesus said to his disciples:] "Do not imagine that I have come
to abolish the Law or the Prophets. I have come not to
abolish but to complete them. I tell you solemnly, till heaven
and earth disappear, not one dot, not one little stroke, shall
disappear from the Law until its purpose is achieved.
Therefore, the man who infringes even one of the least of
these commandments and teaches others to do the same will
be considered the least in the kingdom of heaven; but the man
who keeps them and teaches them will be considered great in
the kingdom of heaven."

MATTHEW 5:17—19

This is a disturbing Gospel passage because Jesus appears to be endorsing the exact observance of rules and regulations as the only way to God. Jesus is not a legalist. Where one of the most solemn obligations for the Jew was observance of the Sabbath, Jesus made the astonishing statement "The Sabbath was made for man, not man for the Sabbath."

The context of this Gospel passage explains its meaning. This passage comes just after the Beatitudes, and the passage that follows it shows how the Beatitudes are, in fact, the fulfillment of the Law.

Virtue lies in motivation rather than in performance. For example, two people may each give one thousand dollars to a charity, which is a good thing to do, but while one may perform the action out of compassion and at great personal sacrifice, the other may do it only because the donation will bring favorable publicity. So Jesus says, "If your virtue goes no deeper than that of the scribes and Pharisees, you will never get into the kingdom of God." He then goes through some of the commandments, showing in what their fulfillment consists.

Fulfillment of the Law consists primarily in an inner attitude of mind and heart rather than in its exact observance. For example, it is not enough to observe the prohibition "Thou shalt not kill." We must live in a state of peace and reconciliation with our brothers and sisters, and love and pray for our enemies.

It is not enough to observe the prohibition "Thou shalt not commit adultery" in our outward actions alone. We must observe it in our hearts as well. It is not enough to observe the prohibition "You must not break your oath." We must learn not to swear by anything outside of us because our yes and our no must express our whole being.

The Law said, "An eye for an eye and a tooth for a tooth," a commandment on which the moralists can make endless observations, such as What if the enemy has already lost an eye or has no teeth? Jesus says that the perfection of this commandment is to offer the wicked man no resistance, and if he hits us on the right cheek, we should offer him our left cheek as well, or if he orders us to go one mile, we should go two miles with him. This is the fulfillment, the perfection of the Law—it demands a radical change in our inner attitudes, not the multiplication of external prescriptions and their scrupulous observance.

It is astonishing how we manage to ignore this teaching of Jesus. Our nuclear deterrence policy, supported by every major political party and by the majority of Christians and Christian leaders, is a contradiction of Jesus' teaching and reveals a deep split in us between what we profess with our lips and what we decide in our hearts.

Prayer

> *Lord, heal the split within us so that we may live the faith in you that we profess. Write your law on our hearts so that all our decisions reflect your compassion for all your creation. We ask you this through Jesus Christ, our Lord. Amen.*

Thursday

JESUS ACCUSED OF BEING DEMONIC

Jeremiah 7:23–28; Psalm 95;
Luke 11:14–23

So tell them this, "Here is the nation that will not listen to the voice of Yahweh its God nor take correction. Sincerity is no more, it has vanished from their mouths."

JEREMIAH 7:28

[Jesus, having been accused of casting out devils through Satan's power,] said to them, "Every kingdom divided against itself is heading for ruin. . . . So too with Satan: if he is divided against himself, how can his kingdom stand? . . . But if it is through the finger of God that I cast out devils, then know that the kingdom of God has overtaken you. . . . He who is not with me is against me; and he who does not gather with me scatters."

LUKE 11:17—18, 20, 23

While many Christians are put off by talk of the devil, demons, or exorcisms, others talk of little else. A healthy spirituality gives more attention to God's presence in all things than to the devil's.

Aldous Huxley's *The Devils of Loudon* is based on fact. A nun in a convent in France was thought to be possessed by the devil. An exorcist was summoned as the possession spread throughout the community. Huxley's thesis is that the nuns were not possessed but because convent life was so repressive, they became possessed, which was considered a perfectly respectable way of escaping from repression and indulging in all kinds of outrageous behavior. This way, the responsibility rested with the devils, not with the individual sisters. By projecting all our evil onto the devil, we avoid having to confront our own sinfulness.

Today, people afflicted with illness are sometimes told by other Christians that their illness is really a spiritual sickness that can be cured only by renouncing some past or present attachment. While it is probably true that many of our bodily ailments are symptomatic of spiritual malaise, this truth can be used to manipulate people; it works on their fears and assures them that they cannot be set free of their afflictions unless they follow the ways that others prescribe.

Scripture speaks of Satan as "the father of lies" and "the accuser," and both descriptions are in today's Gospel passage. If people believe the accusation that Jesus is casting out demons through the devil's power, Jesus can do nothing to disprove the accusation, for all his healing and preaching and goodness can be interpreted as demonic guile. The untrue accusation blinds the believers so that when they are faced with goodness, they can see only evil, and they will as a result feel righteous in condemning the good person, whom they think is evil. We need to pray for an exorcism of our own minds that will cleanse us of all those generalized accusations that can blind us to "that which is of God in everyone."

We also need to ponder "the accuser" in our own minds. Beauty, it is said, is in the eye of the beholder, but so are evil and ugliness. In our judgments of other people, situations, and ourselves, do we usually notice the strengths and the good points, or the defects? What we see and dwell upon we nurture and foster. The communities of one religious superior were always described as outstandingly good. After his death, the superior's biographer commented on this: "The goodness of his communities existed, at first, solely in his pious imagination."

Acknowledging our sins and defects has its place in our lives, but being truly sorry for our sins—a gift of God— always brings hope and a sense of gratitude "to him whose power, working in us, can do infinitely more than we can ask or imagine" (Ephesians 3:20). It is a sound spiritual principle that we should concentrate on our strengths, not on our weaknesses. Wallowing in self-accusation betrays a lack of faith, for we are giving more attention to our weaknesses than to the power of God at work within us.

Prayer

> *Rescue us, Lord, from those destructive places in our minds where darkness dispels all light, where accusation reigns and blinds us to goodness. Cleanse our minds and hearts so that we can always recognize what is of you in ourselves and in every situation. We ask you this through Jesus Christ, our Lord. Amen.*

Friday

Hosea 14:2–10; Psalm 81; Mark 12:28–34

Take all iniquity away so that we may have happiness again and offer you our words of praise. Assyria cannot save us, we will not ride horses any more, or say, "Our God!" to what our own hands have made, for you are the one in whom orphans find compassion.

HOSEA 14:3—4

One of the scribes . . . came up and put a question to [Jesus], "Which is the first of all the commandments?" Jesus replied, "This is the first: Listen, Israel, the Lord our God is the one Lord, and you must love the Lord your God with all your heart, with all your soul, with all your mind, and with all your strength. The second is this: You must love your neighbor as yourself. There is no commandment greater than these."

MARK 12:28—31

"The Lord our God is the one Lord." This belief in the one Lord formed Israel and distinguished her from all her polytheistic neighbors. For the Jew, the gravest sin was idolatry, to worship any god other than the God of Abraham, Isaac, and Jacob. The Exodus account of the golden calf can leave the reader with the impression that idolatry consists of such crude practices and that because we are not so tempted as individuals, as a church, or as a nation, therefore idolatry is not a danger for us. This Hosea passage describes a form of idolatry that is all too familiar to us. Hosea sees Israel's attempts to form alliances with Assyria and her trust in the power of her armed forces as examples of the nation's idolatrous nature, for Israel is putting her trust not in Yahweh but in her own strength and power. Loving the Lord your God with all your heart means living in such a way that God really is our ultimate good and our security and that nothing else that "our hands have made" can take God's place.

We can be idolatrous, in fact, while believing that we are free of idolatry. I must ask myself, "How do I relate to my wealth, possessions, and status in society, to my family and friends, to my health and reputation?" Provided that none of these relationships is threatened, I may feel that I have a healthy relationship with them all, that I am grateful for them but not overly attached. It is when these relationships are threatened that my idolatry is uncovered. The more idolatrous our relationships, the more desperate we will be if any of our securities are threatened, and the more ruthless we will be in preserving them by any means in our power. It is our responsibility to ponder Hosea's message and reflect on whether it has anything to say to us today, both as individuals and as a nation.

"You must love your neighbor as yourself." In the past we have forgotten the "as yourself" part of this commandment because such strong emphasis was placed on self-sacrifice and self-denial that any consideration of one's own needs was considered a weakness and unworthy of a dedicated Christian. This is a destructive teaching and has been the undoing of many generous and committed people. In reaction to this teaching, a modern emphasis has been placed on caring for oneself and one's own development to the extent that an individual has no time, interest, or energy to attend to anyone else. Looking after oneself becomes the first and greatest commandment, the idolatry. This is illustrated in a book called *Reweaving Religious Life* by Mary Jo Leddy, which gives two imaginary obituary notices. The first is for Sister Immaculata, aged eighty-six, who died in 1950, surrounded by her community singing the *Salve Regina*. Sister Immaculata had spent sixty years as an elementary school teacher and will be sadly missed. The other obituary is for Sister Becky, aged eighty-six, who died in 1999 at a sensitivity session, surrounded by her Sisters. Sister Becky had spent one year each as a teacher, a youth minister, a spiritual director, and a nurse. The rest of her life she spent preparing for these ministries.

A way of testing whether our love of self is God-centered or self-centered is to ask of our moods and inner feelings when we review our day, "On whose behalf was I happy, sad, indignant, angry, delighted, and so on, and who is benefiting from what I am doing?"

Prayer

> *Lord, take me by the hand and lead me safely through the tortuous and labyrinthine ways of my own mind so that I may find your path. Rid me of all hidden*

attachments to false idols so that I may be free to love you with all my heart and my neighbor as myself. We ask you this through Jesus Christ, our Lord. Amen.

Saturday

THE PHARISEE AND THE
TAX COLLECTOR

Hosea 5:15–6:6; Psalm 51; Luke 18:9–14

What I want is love, not sacrifice; knowledge of God, not holocausts.

HOSEA 6:6

The Pharisee stood there and said this prayer to himself, "I thank you, God, that I am not grasping, unjust, adulterous like the rest of mankind, and particularly that I am not like this tax collector here. I fast twice a week; I pay tithes on all I get." The tax collector stood some distance away, not daring even to raise his eyes to heaven; but he beat his breast and said, "God, be merciful to me, a sinner." This man, I tell you, went home again at rights with God; the other did not. For everyone who exalts himself will be humbled, but the man who humbles himself will be exalted.

LUKE 18:11–14

It is natural for us to feel right with ourselves if we have acted justly or generously, if we have prayed, or if we have fasted, so in the story of the Pharisee and the tax collector, are we to believe that Jesus is condemning us for experiencing the inner peace that comes of right action?

Tax collectors were employed to collect taxes on behalf of the Romans, a profitable occupation for the tax collectors but one that earned them the contempt of their own people. The tax collector in the parable may well have been guilty of all those sins that the Pharisee attributed to him and the rest of humanity, and he was probably also a nonpracticing Jew, neither paying taxes nor fasting. The Pharisee is therefore morally superior and, in religious practice, religiously superior to the tax collector, so what is wrong with his acknowledging this superiority and thanking God for it? We need to ask this question of ourselves and see what answer we give.

The parable is introduced with the sentence "[Jesus] spoke the following parable to some people who prided themselves on being virtuous and despised everyone else." What Jesus is condemning is the Pharisee's sense of superiority, which leads the Pharisee to despise the tax collector.

A few verses after this parable, Luke relates the story of the rich young man who addresses Jesus as "Good Master," to which Jesus replies, "Why do you call me good? No one is good but God alone." The Pharisee fails, in spite of his correct behavior and faithful observance, because he considers himself the author and owner of his own virtue. Because the Pharisee finds the tax collector so lamentably lacking in virtue, he will feel fully justified in his contempt for the tax collector. In Jesus' thinking, this is a far greater sin than those that the Pharisee attributes to the tax collector and the rest of humankind.

The tax collector is aware of his own failure. He neither appeals to any good he may have done nor makes any attempt to justify himself but abandons himself to the mercy of God. He knows that "no one is good but God alone." And Jesus said: "This man went home at rights with God; the other did not."

This is a profoundly important parable, and the more religious we are, the more we need to ponder it.

God alone is the author of any good we may have done or may ever do. God's ways are not our ways, nor are his judgments our judgments. God may well be much closer to the nonchurchgoing moral reprobate than he is to the person who appears to be a model of rectitude in the church.

It is not only the tax collector whom the Pharisee will despise. He will also despise and try to disown those aspects of himself that are akin to those of the tax collector. As he considers himself the author of all his own virtue and goodness, when he is confronted with his own darkness, he will either try to deny it or will be tempted to despair.

From this parable it seems that what matters to God is not so much our achievements and observances but the tendency of the sheepdog part of ourselves to turn to him in the depths of ourselves and acknowledge that he alone is good. It is then that we can pray that he may be God to us and through us.

Prayer

> *Save us, Lord, from the idol of self-righteousness. Help us to know you, source of all goodness, and to trust always in your mercy for us all. We ask you this through Jesus Christ, our Lord. Amen.*

Sunday

JESUS, LIGHT OF THE WORLD

1 Samuel 16:1–13; Psalm 23; John 9:1–41

[Jesus said,] "I am the light of the world." Having said this, he spat on the ground, made a paste with the spittle, put this over the eyes of the blind man, and said to him, "Go and wash in the Pool of Siloam" (a name that means "sent"). So the blind man went off and washed himself, and came away with his sight restored. . . . Then some of the Pharisees said, "This man cannot be from God: he does not keep the sabbath." . . . The Jews would not believe that the man had been blind and had gained his sight, without first sending for his parents and asking them. . . . His parents answered, "We know he is our son and we know he was born blind." . . . [The man born blind said,] "Ever since the world began it is unheard of for anyone to open the eyes of a man who was born blind; if this man were not from God, he couldn't do a thing." "Are you trying to teach us," they replied, "and you a sinner through and through, since you were born!" . . . Jesus said, "It is for judgment that I have come into this world, so that those without sight may see and those with sight turn blind." Hearing this, some Pharisees

who were present said to him, "We are not blind, surely?"
Jesus replied: "Blind? If you were, you would not be guilty,
but since you say, 'We see,' your guilt remains."

JOHN 9:5—7, 16, 18—20, 32—34, 39—41

John makes it very clear that Jesus' miracles are not simply extraordinary physical happenings but signs that point beyond a physical cure to a truth that affects all people of all times. Jesus gives light to a blind man, a sign that he is the light of the world. The Pharisees' reaction also points beyond their own group, their own religion, and their own time, for the blindness that afflicts them can manifest itself in people of any religion as well as in those who have no religion.

The Pharisees refuse to accept that Jesus could have performed this miracle through the power of God because he performed the miracle on the Sabbath. It is sobering to think that attachment to a religious belief or observance, while good in itself, can not only blind its devotees to the presence of God but can also lead them to try to get rid of that presence.

We need to reflect on this phenomenon in our own lives, on how our inherited belief system, whether religious or secular, can blind us to the truth of things and lead us to act destructively while we are convinced that we are acting correctly or even religiously. The less we examine our belief system, the more rigid it is likely to be, and the more ruthlessly we will apply it. Such crude belief systems always oversimplify matters, which is part of their attraction.

If we really do believe in Christ, light of the world, then we need to examine our own beliefs and attitudes: our racism, sexism, and militarism; our feelings toward people of other Christian denominations, other religions,

WEEK FIVE

or no religion; and our feelings toward people of cultures or backgrounds that are different from our own. Our failure to examine ourselves in this way can lead us to the most inhuman behavior. Even today, some people still defend the deliberate bombing of innocent civilians in World War II and the dropping of the atomic bombs on Hiroshima and Nagasaki. The blindness of the Pharisees still afflicts us.

But the healing power of Jesus is still with us. If we look to him, we will begin to see more clearly that Jesus is living not just in the minds of pious believers but in the reality of every human life. If we look to him, we will begin to see more clearly that which is of God in everyone we meet and realize that when we condemn or exclude any individual, group, category, or class of people, we condemn and exclude ourselves.

Prayer

> *Jesus, light of the world, be the light and the joy of my life. Dispel the darkness of my fears and break down the barriers of my prejudice so that I may recognize that which is of you in everyone I meet and live grateful for your presence within and among us. Amen.*

Monday

GOD'S HEALING POWER

Isaiah 65:17–21; Psalm 30; John 4:43–54

*[Yahweh says this:] Now I create new heavens and a new
earth, and the past will not be remembered. . . . Be glad and
rejoice for ever and ever for what I am creating, because I
now create Jerusalem "Joy" and her people "Gladness." I
shall rejoice over Jerusalem and exult in my people.*

ISAÏAH 65:17–19

*[Jesus] went again to Cana in Galilee. . . . Now there was a
court official there whose son was ill at Capernaum and,
hearing that Jesus had arrived in Galilee from Judaea, he
went and asked him to come and cure his son as he was at the
point of death. . . . "Go home," said Jesus, "your son will
live." The man believed what Jesus had said and started on
his way; and while he was still on the journey back his servants met him with the news that his boy was alive. He asked
them when the boy had begun to recover. "The fever left him
yesterday," they said, "at the seventh hour." The father
realized that this was exactly the time when Jesus had said,
"Your son will live"; and he and all his household believed.
This was the second sign given by Jesus.*

JOHП 4:46–47, 50–54

Jesus performs the miracle related in the Gospel passage at the request of a court official, who is probably a pagan, on behalf of the official's son. The official begins to trust Jesus, and at the moment he does so, his son recovers; later, the whole household comes to believe. The miracle is a sign of Jesus' power over sickness and death, a power that he exercises on request, even, as in this case, at the request of a pagan. Jesus demands faith of the official but not of his son, whom he cures at his father's request. The official's faith affects his whole household.

We read the Gospels in order to put ourselves in touch with God now. Imagine that this scene is happening now and that we are not simply spectators but active participants in it. One value of imaginative contemplation is its power to put us in touch with the reality in which we live. The God who held Jesus in being and who healed people through Jesus is the God now holding you and me in being. God wants our healing and health even more than we do. If we assent to this truth with our heads only, we are unlikely to experience healing. If we can imagine Jesus before us, as in this scene, and can present ourselves and our needs to him, we are more likely to break through to the reality of God's healing powers enveloping us. Trust opens us to these healing powers. That is why Jesus keeps saying, "Your faith has saved you, go in peace."

In this miracle, healing comes to the son through the intercession of his father. We pray for our own healing, but we should also pray for the gift of healing. We think of healing as a very rare and spectacular kind of gift that is granted to a few chosen people. While it is true that some people have remarkable healing gifts, every Christian is called to be a healer in some way, for the life of Christ is a healing life. Being a good listener, being patient and tolerant, having a sense of humor, being efficient, being interested, and being willing to waste time with people are just a few of the many ways in which we can be healers to one another.

Our own struggles toward inner peace and harmony are never purely private concerns, although they may seem to be. In life, we are all exposed to destructive forces, and we can react to them in different ways. We can either absorb the destructive forces, intensifying the destructiveness in our own hearts and sending them out with more destructive power than before, or we can absorb the violence, as Jesus did, transform it within us, and send it out in the form of forgiveness, blessing, and kindness. An inner act of pure love is more effective and creative than any amount of external activity we can pursue. When the Final Judgment comes, I am sure we will all be surprised to discover who the real heroes and heroines have been, who sustained the world and saved it from destruction. They will probably be obscure people with healing hearts, who absorbed bitterness, violence, and disillusionment but transformed them in their hearts to generate a spirit of forgiveness, gentleness, and hope.

Prayer

> *Lord, deepen our trust in the healing power of your Spirit working within us and through us, absorbing the violence and hatred and transforming it into mercy and love toward ourselves and toward others. We ask you this through Jesus Christ, our Lord. Amen.*

Tuesday

LIVING WATER

Ezekiel 47:1–12; Psalm 46; John 5:1–16

[Ezekiel's vision of the water flowing from the temple.] "The man went to the east holding his measuring line and measured off a thousand cubits; he then made me wade across the stream; the water reached my ankles. . . . He measured off another thousand and made me wade across again; the water reached my waist. He measured off another thousand; it was now a river which I could not cross; the stream had swollen and was now deep water, a river impossible to cross. . . . He took me further, then brought me back to the bank of the river. . . . He said, "This water flows east down to the Arabah and to the sea; and flowing into the sea it makes its waters wholesome. Wherever the river flows, all living creatures teeming in it will live. Fish will be very plentiful, for wherever the water goes it brings health, and life teems wherever the river flows. . . . The marshes and lagoons, however, will not become wholesome, but will remain salt. Along the river, on either bank, will grow every kind of fruit tree with leaves that never wither and fruit that never fails."

EZEKİEL 47:3—6, 8—9, II—I2

[Jesus] said, "Do you want to be well again?" "Sir," replied the sick man, "I have no one to put me into the pool when the water is disturbed. . . ." Jesus said, "Get up, pick up your sleeping mat and walk." The man was cured at once.

JOHΠ 5:6—9

Imagination is a much-neglected faculty. Images are much more likely to move us than words are. For example, I can read with my mind or with my imagination Ezekiel's vision of the river flowing from the temple, and the effect on me will be different with each. When I read it with my mind, I may remember all the details and find them interesting, and I may even look up a biblical commentary on the passage and try to locate the river on a map, but my feelings will not be engaged by the imagery. The images do not linger in my consciousness, nor do they affect my mood or behavior in any noticeable way during the day. If I read the vision with my imagination, the effect will be very different, as you can discover for yourself.

Imagine yourself wading across the stream the first time, as in the vision, and feel the water flow over your ankles. This water that you feel is the life of God. Early baptismal fonts were sunk into the ground so that those being baptized could feel themselves entering into the death and life of Christ. "You have been taught that when we were baptized in Christ Jesus we were baptized in his death; in other words, when we were baptized we went into the tomb with him and joined him in death, so that as Christ was raised from the dead by the Father's glory, we too might live a new life" (Romans 6:3–4).

Baptism is a Greek word that means "to plunge into," so by imagining yourself wading across the water flowing from the temple, you are in fact getting in touch with your own reality, your own baptism, your own being plunged into the life of God.

As you wade across the stream a second time, up to your knees, and a third time, up to your waist, surrender each part of your body to God as the waters envelop you. Offer, too, your senses, your inner moods and feelings, your mental attitudes and ways of thinking, and your memories to the cleansing, purifying, and energizing power of God's life.

As you step deeper into the water, you lose your footing, and the stream carries you. Feel the flow of the stream and yourself moving with it, the healing waters enlivening you and bringing life wherever they flow. As the stream carries you, look back at the marshes and lagoons, salty and dead because they are cut off from the river's flow. Then pray to know the reality of these images in your own life, in those times when you can let God be God in you and through you, and the enlivening effect this has on you. Pray to know too the times when you resist the living stream, preferring the salt marshes and lagoons, and note the effect that this has on you and on those around you. Through the circumstances of our lives God is nudging us and beckoning us to live in the stream of his life, not in the lagoons and marshes of our own kingdoms.

Prayer

> *God, source of all life and goodness, free us from false images of ourselves and of you and from every form of self-preoccupation, whether of self-praise or self-blame, so that our lives may flow in the stream of your life. We ask you this through Jesus Christ, our Lord. Amen.*

Wednesday

AT-ONE-MENT

Isaiah 49:8–15; Psalm 145; John 5:17–30

*For Zion was saying, "Yahweh has abandoned me, the
Lord has forgotten me." Does a woman forget her baby
at the breast, or fail to cherish the child of her womb? Yet
even if these forget, I will never forget you.*

ISAIAH 49:14—15

*[Jesus answered,] "My Father goes on working, and so
do I." But that only made the Jews even more intent on
killing him, because, not content with breaking the sabbath,
he spoke of God as his own Father, and so made himself
God's equal. To this accusation Jesus replied: "I tell you
most solemnly, the Son can do nothing by himself; he can
do only what he sees the Father doing. . . . I can do nothing
by myself; I can only judge as I am told to judge, and my
judging is just, because my aim is to do not my own will,
but the will of him who sent me."*

JOHN 5:17—19, 30

When we look at Jesus' life, we are in a sense also looking at ourselves, for the pattern of his life is to be the pattern of our own. "In your minds you must be the same as Christ Jesus" (Philippians 2:5).

What characterizes Jesus' life and distinguishes him from every great religious leader is his relationship with God, whom he calls "Abba," the child's "Dad" or "Daddy." Luke's Gospel contains the only recorded words of Jesus in his first thirty years, the twelve-year-old Jesus' reply to his mother after she had lost him for three days: "Did you not know that I must be about my Father's affairs?" This core relationship to "Abba" pervades all the teachings and actions in Jesus' public life, culminating in his agony ("Not my will, but thine be done") and in his death on the cross ("Into thy hands I commend my spirit").

Jesus prays that his followers should have this same relationship with God: "Father, may they be one in us, as you are in me and I am in you" (John 17:21).

How did Jesus think of "Abba," with whom his whole life is identified? The parables give us a clue. One of Jesus' favorite parables is that of the king who holds a wedding feast for his son. The king's one desire is that as many people as possible should enjoy the celebration. When some of those invited do not turn up, the king tells the servants to go into the hedgerows and byways and bring them all in, lame and blind. In Matthew's Gospel the servants are told to bring in everyone, "wicked and good alike." God is presented here and in so many of the other parables as a God of prodigal generosity, foolish by our standards because he readily forgives one debtor ten thousand talents, the equivalent of seven million dollars. When that same debtor imprisons his debtor for a paltry sum, he is put back in prison until he pays the last penny. God, who is prodigally generous, cannot stand stinginess, as we see in the Dives and Lazarus parable.

This life of God manifests itself in the teachings and actions of Jesus, culminating at the Last Supper, when Jesus takes a piece of bread, blesses it, breaks it, and gives it to the apostles, saying "This is me, given for you. Do this in my memory," an instruction that does not simply mean "Keep repeating this ritual action," but "Let this action be the pattern of your life too, as it is of mine."

Many people have difficulty in approaching God as "Father." If this is difficult for you, change "Father" to "Mother" or, as the Song of Songs does, to "lover." Use whatever is helpful. The reality, God, is more important than the actual name with which you address God, who is love and is "closer to me than I am to myself."

Prayer

> *Lord, free us of all destructive fear and anxiety, and still our hearts and minds so that in pondering your word in Scripture and contemplating the life of Jesus we may recognize his Spirit dwelling within us and drawing us to be at one with you and with all creation. We ask you this through Jesus Christ, our Lord. Amen.*

Thursday

IDOLATRY AND APPROVAL

Exodus 32:7–14; Psalm 106; John 5:31–47

*Then Yahweh spoke to Moses, "Go down now, because your
people whom you brought out of Egypt have apostatized.
They have been quick to leave the way I marked out for
them; they have made themselves a calf of molten metal
and have worshiped it and offered it sacrifice. 'Here is your
God, Israel,' they have cried, 'who brought you up from the
land of Egypt.'" . . . But Moses pleaded with Yahweh his
God. . . . So Yahweh relented and did not bring on his
people the disaster he had threatened.*

EXODUS 32:7–8, 11, 14

*You study the scriptures, believing that in them you have
eternal life; now these same scriptures testify to me, and yet
you refuse to come to me for life! . . . You have no love of
God in you. . . . How can you believe, since you look to one
another for approval and are not concerned with the approval
that comes from the one God?*

JOHN 5:39–40, 42, 44

The Jews study the Scriptures in faith, yet they do not recognize Jesus, the fulfillment of the Scriptures, standing before them. John was not writing to let his readers know how wrong the Jews were because most of his readers would have been Jewish. He was writing about spiritual blindness, which afflicts Christians and Jews alike.

It is of the nature of spiritual blindness that those afflicted by it are convinced that they are seeing clearly. They are like the man who got very drunk and sat on a wineglass. He thought that he had treated his wounds before he went to bed, but the next morning he found the wounds untreated and a neat pattern of adhesive strips laid across a mirror on the floor.

Jesus gives two causes of spiritual blindness: first, "You have no love of God in you," and second, "You look to one another for approval and are not concerned with the approval that comes from the one God."

Single-mindedness is generally considered a virtue, but it may be a vice if the single-mindedness excludes love. I once heard about an experiment that was administered to students who were studying for the ministry. The students were visiting a hospital, where they were given a memory test. Someone would read them a story in one room, and then they would proceed to another room where they were to repeat the story to someone else as word-perfectly as possible. They were read the parable of the Good Samaritan, and in the corridor between the two rooms a patient was lying in pain and crying for help. The single-minded students, so intent on remembering the parable, ignored the patient. We are all liable to this loveless single-mindedness, which can appear in an especially virulent form in religious people. "You who travel over sea and land to make a single proselyte, and when you have him you make him twice as fit for hell as you are" (Matthew 23:15).

Loveless single-mindedness will win us the approval, support, and encouragement of all that are similarly afflicted. Surrounded by such support and approval, we will not be concerned with earning the approval of the one God. In their blindness, the Israelites worshiped the golden calf. We do not have a golden calf, but we do have market forces, a deadly virus that slips into every aspect of our lives, eventually taking over, subjecting every human value to its inhuman dictates. No area of life—be it education, research, physical and mental health care, environmentalism, entertainment, leisure, or communications—is impervious to its poison. Both the singer and the song must be regulated according to "market forces," which sounds like some harmless, objective criterion but in fact is the poisonous growth of greedy hearts. In the language of market forces, the soul, not being quantifiable, does not count. With the new gospel of prosperity, religion itself is being used very successfully to encourage the worship of market forces. "Invest your money with the Lord Jesus and you will have a rich return, tenfold and a hundredfold." Yes, religion can be very profitable, and when it becomes so, it masks the face of God much more effectively than any atheist can ever do.

Prayer

> *Lord, give us eyes to see you, ears to hear you, and a loving heart to recognize you in everyone we meet. Save us from delighting in anything that does not*

bear the imprint of your love and goodness and deliver us individually and nationally from the idolatry of market forces. We ask you this through Jesus Christ, our Lord. Amen.

Friday

VIOLENCE

Wisdom 2:12–22; Psalm 34; John 7:1–30

*[The godless say to themselves, with their misguided rea-
soning,] "Let us lie in wait for the virtuous man, since he
annoys us and opposes our way of life. . . . The very sight of
him weighs our spirits down. . . . Let us test him with cruelty
and with torture, and thus explore this gentleness of his
and put his endurance to the proof. Let us condemn him to
a shameful death since he will be looked after—we have his
word for it."*

WISDOM 2:12, 14, 19–20

*After this Jesus stayed in Galilee; he could not stay in Judaea,
because the Jews were out to kill him.*

JOHN 7:1

How did Jesus become so unpopular that his own people
were out to kill him? The Gospels present him as
attractive and compassionate. Only the very evil, we
think, could possibly hate such a man. Because the Jewish
leaders are presented as wanting to kill Jesus, the conclusion

drawn is that they must be malicious. Although this is a thoroughly illogical conclusion, it has infected Christian consciousness and brought misery to generations of Jews, who have been labeled by Christians as "Christ-killers." It was the Christians themselves who perpetrated the very evils of which they accused the Jewish people. Jesus identified himself with every human being in his description of the Final Judgment, "in so far as you did this to one of the least of these brothers of mine, you did it to me" (Matthew 25:40). Our relationship with God is expressed in our relationships with one another. Whatever we do to one another we are also doing to God. The Jewish people did not crucify Jesus; he is crucified by any of us whenever we violate another human being.

There is a latent violence, a desire to destroy, in all of us. Violence, once unleashed, is like fire, devouring and destroying everything it encounters. Many of the taboos and customs of ancient societies, such as the Jewish scapegoat, who is symbolically laden with Israel's sins and driven into the desert to be destroyed, are attempts to contain and limit the danger of raging violence. The Greek historian Thucydides wrote that the first casualty in war is truth, for in war, cruelty becomes a virtue. We have seen the horrors of unleashed violence in our century. We all deplore it, throwing up our hands in horror, and then proceed to restore law and order by more violence. By its nature, violence is imitative and contagious. Those who counter violence with violence have been infected by the violence they deplore and are adding to it. World War I was to be the war to end all wars. The armed violence ended on Armistice Day in 1918, but the seeds of violence remained in human hearts and erupted again in 1939.

Since the end of World War II in 1945, there have been over two hundred wars, most of them in Third World countries, where the superpowers continued their conflict. Now that the Communist bloc has collapsed and the violence of a totalitarian regime has ceased, ancient animosities within the former Communist bloc countries have been revived, and new violence threatens to erupt.

Every conflict in which our own countries are engaged is always justified by the state, and while the church does not fully endorse such conflicts, neither does it condemn them. Any who question our national rectitude or our need to preserve peace by violent means are immediately pilloried. Dorothy Day once asked, "Is there a difference between throwing innocent people into ovens and throwing ovens at innocent people?" All political parties and most church leaders believe that threatening to throw ovens at innocent people is legitimate. To hold a contrary opinion is considered politically disreputable and a sign of unfitness to govern. It is of the nature of evil, as the Wisdom reading states, to corrupt the mind so that what is good and creative is considered dangerous and destructive.

The seeds of violence are in our own minds and hearts. They are nurtured by every form of prejudice and strengthened and sustained by our fears. They infect every aspect of our lives, turning even our religious beliefs into instruments of violence.

Prayer

> *O God, eradicate from our minds and hearts the hidden roots of violence and destruction. Infect our minds and hearts with the gentleness of your Son, so that we may*

learn to counter violence with blessing, hatred with love, and cruelty with kindness. We ask you this through Jesus Christ, our Lord. Amen.

Saturday

WHAT IS TRUTH?

Jeremiah 11:18–20; Psalm 7; John 7:40–52

Several people who had been listening [to Jesus] said, "Surely he must be the prophet," and some said, "He is the Christ," but others said, "Would the Christ be from Galilee? Does not scripture say that the Christ must be descended from David and come from the town of Bethlehem?" So the people could not agree about him. . . . The police went back to the chief priests and Pharisees who said to them, "Why haven't you brought him?" The police replied, "There has never been anybody who has spoken like him." "So," the Pharisees answered, "you have been led astray as well? Have any of the authorities believed in him? Any of the Pharisees? This rabble knows nothing about the Law—they are damned." One of them, Nicodemus . . . said to them, "But surely the Law does not allow us to pass judgement on a man without giving him a hearing and discovering what he is about?" To this they answered, "Are you a Galilean too? Go into the matter, and see for yourself: prophets do not come out of Galilee."

JOHN 7:40—43, 45—52

During his trial before Pilate, Jesus said, "I was born for this, I came into the world for this: to bear witness to the truth; and all who are on the side of truth listen to my voice." In contemplating and reflecting on Jesus' life and death, we can begin to see more clearly the truth and untruth in our own lives.

In this Gospel passage, truth and untruth are in conflict. Whenever the truth is declared, it is countered with a generalization: "Prophets do not come out of Galilee," and "How can it be true—none of the authorities believe in him?" and "The people who declare him to be a prophet are an ignorant rabble." The people making these generalizations do so with great confidence, citing their status and their opponents' lack of status to back up their assertions.

The tyrannical rule of untruth continues on in every individual, nation, and aspect of life, and each of us is liable to be both its perpetrators and its victims.

Our political system encourages us to think in generalizations, to accept or reject policies not because they are true or untrue in themselves but because they are favored or opposed by the other party. With the demise of Communism, tyrannical governments suffered a serious blow, now no longer able to use the label "Communist" to condemn any policies opposed to their own.

As our society becomes more complex and technological, opportunities for the tyrannical rule of untruth increase. Teachers are particularly susceptible to the temptation to control truth, to form young minds in the templates of their own prejudices, and to stamp heavily on their students' attempts at original thought while assuring them of their inferiority. We become increasingly dependent on the expert, who tells us what to eat, what to wear, what medicines and surgeries we need, and how and what to think. The few make large profits by robbing the many of self-trust and self-confidence in the truth they discover for themselves.

The chief priests' and Pharisees' attitude toward Jesus keeps recurring in the history of Christianity. Churches and sects split off from one another in an attempt to recover the freedom of truth, and many end up more authoritarian than the parent body ever was. In your own experience of church, how far have you been encouraged to be critical, to discover for yourself? How often have you had the experience of being listened to in your church or encouraged to express what you really think and feel without being judged or disapproved of in any way? Have you spent time listening to others in this way? Have you felt nervous at some of the ideas they express? How have you reacted?

Prayer

> *Spirit of truth, permeate my mind and heart so that I can listen with discernment. Deliver me from every form of superiority that deafens me to you in the cries of the poor and powerless. I ask you this through Jesus Christ, our Lord. Amen.*

Sunday

NEW LIFE

Ezekiel 37:12–14; Psalm 130;
Romans 8:8–11; John 11:1–45

Say to them, "The Lord Yahweh says this: . . . I mean to
raise you from your graves, my people. . . . I shall put my
spirit in you, and you will live."

EZEKIEL 37:12, 14

If the Spirit of him who raised Jesus from the dead is
living in you, then he who raised Jesus from the dead will
give life to your own mortal bodies through his Spirit
living in you.

ROMANS 8:11

Jesus said: "I am the resurrection. If anyone believes in me,
even though he dies he will live, and whoever lives and
believes in me will never die. . . ." "Lazarus, here! Come
out!" The dead man came out, his feet and hands bound
with bands of stuff and a cloth around his face. Jesus said
to them, "Unbind him, let him go free."

JOHN 11:25–26, 43–44

The theme of today's reading is new life, which is promised in Ezekiel and realized in Jesus' raising of the dead Lazarus.

This is a powerful theme, so powerful that it can numb rather than enliven, bewilder rather than enlighten. It is difficult for us to engage with ideas that are beyond our experience, so we tip our mental hats to the phrases "life after death," "eternal life," and "resurrection of the body," neither denying their possible truth nor letting them affect us while we get on with the messy business of day-to-day life. But if these themes are important, they must be important for us now.

The British public is not noted for its interest in theology, yet when the former bishop of Durham raised questions about the meaning of the Resurrection, he was faced with indignant outcries and accusations of heresy. We would prefer him to leave the Resurrection alone, as a secure article of faith that is to be accepted but not explored.

When national controversy over the nature of the Resurrection was raging, one writer pleaded with Christians to stop trying to prove that we will have a material body after death and to concentrate instead on the chance that we might not have a material body now. The mystery is not only in the future: the mystery is also now. Each of us is a mystery, a conglomerate of billions of cells, each of which is a mystery in itself. We are living mysteries, our conscious minds grasping only the tiniest fraction of the reality that we are. Pondering the mystery of our being can open our minds to Jesus' message: "I am the resurrection," and help us to escape the narrow prison of our own thoughts, ideas, and assumptions to live in a less fearful and more hopeful reality that is not just for us in the future but also for us now.

Imaginatively contemplating the raising of Lazarus can put us in touch with our present reality. Watch the miracle happen and then become like Lazarus in the tomb, bound in grave clothes, trapped in total darkness. Hear the footsteps and the voice saying, "I am the resurrection," and hear the stone being moved away from the entrance of the tomb. Hear Jesus calling you by name and saying, "Arise, come forth."

This can be a most revealing exercise that can affect each one of us differently. We may find ourselves saying, "Thanks, Lord, but I prefer to stay where I am," or we may find we are afraid, or unable, to move, or we may suddenly become aware of how tomb-like our present way of life really is. The exercise may arouse in us a sense of hope and rekindle a longing for freedom that has, perhaps, been buried for years, or it may help us see that our present circumstances are less hopeless than we had thought. Whatever happens, speak with God about it and ask him how you should react.

The reality for all of us is that God is calling us out of death into life, continuously and in all the events of our lives. How we respond now to this call determines how we will be in the future. So speak to God who is now calling you. Ask yourself, "How have I responded to him in the past? How am I now responding? How do I want to respond in the future?" Then you can leave the details of your future safely in his hands.

Prayer

> *God, source of all life and love, free us from the tombs in which our fears, past hurts, and resentments imprison us, and draw us into your eternal life now and forever. We ask you this through Jesus Christ, our Lord. Amen.*

Monday

DO NOT JUDGE

Daniel 13:1–62; Psalm 23; John 8:1–11

The scribes and Pharisees brought a woman along who had been caught committing adultery; and making her stand there in full view of everybody, they said to Jesus, "Master, this woman was caught in the very act of committing adultery, and Moses has ordered us in the Law to condemn women like this to death by stoning. What have you to say?" They asked him this as a test, looking for something to use against him. But Jesus bent down and started writing on the ground with his finger. As they persisted with their question, he looked up and said, "If there is one of you who has not sinned, let him be the first to throw a stone at her." Then he bent down and wrote on the ground again. When they heard this they went away one by one, beginning with the eldest, until Jesus was left alone with the woman, who remained standing there. He looked up and said, "Woman, where are they? Has no one condemned you?" "No one, sir," she replied. "Neither do I condemn you," said Jesus, "go away and don't sin any more."

JOHN 8:3–11

This passage does not appear in some of the early Gospel manuscripts, presumably because it was thought to be untrue or, if true, unsuitable reading for Christians.

Jesus says, "Go and sin no more." He is not condoning adultery, but neither does he condemn the woman. He is practicing his own instructions to "judge no one."

Of all the difficult demands Jesus makes of his followers, one of the most difficult and most ignored is his command to judge no one. Today's Gospel reading is not about adultery but about condemnation. Adultery can destroy in very obvious ways, but condemnation can be even more destructive, especially when it masquerades as righteousness.

In this passage, John presents the scribes and Pharisees as being pleased, both at catching the woman and at the chance to test Jesus. We all possess the unpleasant trait that causes us to delight in the misfortune of others provided that we are unscathed ourselves. The Germans call this delight in another's misfortune schadenfreude, a characteristic that keeps the tabloids selling by the millions.

The roots of Schadenfreude go deeper than sins of the flesh. We are anxious creatures, and our deepest fear is that of annihilation, of being literally a nobody. One way to counter this fear is to feel superior to someone in some respect. The belief that "someone is inferior, therefore I am superior!" results in ruthless and bitter struggles in society, often among the poorest people.

Society, whether of church or state, organizes itself in some kind of caste or class system to ensure this superiority. Nations believe their survival depends on having an enemy of some kind, and in rallying a nation, nothing is more effective than going to war. Our educational system, with its emphasis on competition rather than cooperation, and our economy, with its emphasis on "market forces," both nurture this existential anxiety so that our survival depends on having an advantage over someone, on doing better than others rather than cooperating with them. We are caught up in a whole web of values that stems from this fear of annihilation, making war, violence, oppression, and exploitation inevitable.

Jesus said, "Let the person without sin cast the first stone." We can never assess the inner guilt of others, because we cannot know the past influences that are now affecting them or the pressures that afflict them. We can say that their behavior is objectively wrong, immoral, or illegal, but we can never know their inner guilt before God. The only person we should judge is ourselves. If we bring ourselves before God and acknowledge our guilt, he will never refuse forgiveness. We must never, therefore, condemn or refuse to forgive another person in our hearts, for in refusing to forgive them, we are refusing to let God be the God of forgiveness to us.

Prayer

Lord, you said, "Let the person without sin cast the first stone." Show us our own sin and your mercy so that we may always be gentle and never condemn others in our hearts. We ask you this through Jesus Christ, our Lord. Amen.

Tuesday

LOOKING AT THE CROSS

Numbers 21:4–9; Psalm 102; John 8:21–30

[The Israelites] spoke against God and against Moses, "Why did you bring us out of Egypt to die in this wilderness? For there is neither bread nor water here; we are sick of this unsatisfying food." At this God sent fiery serpents among the people; their bite brought death to many in Israel. . . . Moses interceded for the people, and Yahweh answered him, "Make a fiery serpent and put it on a standard. If anyone is bitten and looks at it, he shall live."

ПUMBERS 21:5—8

Jesus said: "When you have lifted up the Son of Man, then you will know that I am He and that I do nothing of myself: what the Father has taught me is what I preach; he who sent me is with me, and has not left me to myself, for I always do what pleases him."

JOHП 8:28—29

The story of the fiery serpent is strange, for it presents an unpleasant God who answers his children's complaints of hunger and thirst by sending fiery serpents that have lethal bites. Jesus must have found it an odd story too, for in Luke's Gospel he asks, "What father among you would hand his son a snake instead of a fish?" Yet it is the image of the fiery serpent, raised on a standard, that saves the stricken who look upon it. Whatever the origins of the story, the bronze serpent raised on a standard prefigures Jesus raised up on the cross and drawing all creation to him. "God wanted all perfection to be found in him and all things to be reconciled through him and for him, everything in heaven and everything on earth, when he made peace by his death on the cross" (Colossians 1:19–20).

A magical element is present in the original story because we can see no causality between looking at a bronze serpent and being healed of snakebite. Is the cross a saving sign in the same magical way? On Good Friday many churches celebrate a ceremony called "Veneration of the Cross," in which the congregation is invited to make some gesture of reverence to the cross: kissing it or bowing, kneeling, or genuflecting before it. We can treat the cross as if it is magical, as though a mere bow, genuflection, or kiss can heal all the damage we have done to others and to ourselves, assuring us an eternity of bliss in the bargain.

The salvation that Jesus offers is not magic. As we have seen in so many of our readings, the Old Testament prophets are forever railing against empty religious gestures: "Rend your hearts; not your garments," "Let justice flow like water, integrity like an unfailing stream."

A cross is a sign. In itself it can effect nothing. Its value is in its ability to point to a reality, the reality of God becoming one of us in Jesus. Jesus died two thousand years ago in a once-for-all historic happening that cannot be repeated, but the Spirit who lived in Jesus and raised him from the dead now lives in us. We look on the cross to remind ourselves of who we are, of our origins with God, who "before the world was, had us in mind," and of our destination, returning to God, which we make not alone but in Christ, through whom we are in relationship with every other human being and all of creation. The vertical part of the cross represents our relationship with God, whom we can find only through the horizontal part, which represents our relationship with one another.

Salvation is letting the Spirit of Christ be the Spirit of Christ in us and through us. We cannot be saved no matter how often we look at and venerate the cross or receive the sacraments unless we are letting the Spirit of Jesus reign in us and through us. The Spirit of Jesus is the Spirit of forgiveness, the Spirit of nonviolent resistance, the Spirit that enables us to love our enemies and bless those who persecute us.

It is good for us just to gaze at Jesus on the cross, as though we were there at the moment of his dying, and then ask ourselves, "What response have I made? What response am I now making? How do I want to respond in the future?"

Prayer

> *Help us to gaze at you on the cross so that we may recognize your Spirit living in our hearts, the Spirit of peace and reconciliation, the Spirit of forgiveness and love for our enemies. We ask you this through Jesus Christ, our Lord. Amen.*

Wednesday

WHERE IS SALVATION?

Daniel 3:14–28, 52–56; John 8:31–42

[King Nebuchadnezzar] gave orders for the furnace to be made seven times hotter than usual, and commanded certain stalwarts from his army to bind Shadrach, Meshach and Abednego and throw them into the burning fiery furnace. . . . Then King Nebuchadnezzar sprang to his feet in amazement. He said to his advisers, "Did we not have these three men thrown bound into the fire?" They replied, "Certainly, O king." "But," he went on, "I can see four men walking about freely in the heart of the fire without coming to any harm. And the fourth looks like a son of the gods." . . . Nebuchadnezzar exclaimed, "Blessed be the God of Shadrach, Meshach and Abednego: he has sent his angel to rescue his servants who, putting their trust in him, defied the order of the king, and preferred to forfeit their bodies rather than serve or worship any god but their own."

DANIEL 3:19–22, 24–25, 28

Jesus said: "If you make my word your home you will indeed be my disciples, you will learn the truth and the

*truth shall make you free." They answered, "We are
descended from Abraham and we have never been the
slaves of anyone." . . . They repeated, "Our father is
Abraham." Jesus said to them: "If you were Abraham's
children, you would do as Abraham did. As it is, you want
to kill me when I tell you the truth as I have learned it
from God; that is not what Abraham did. What you are
doing is what your father does."*

JOHN 8:31–33, 39–41

Many scholars believe that the Book of Daniel was written
between 167 and 164 B.C., when the Jews were suffering
under the rule of the Greek king Antiochus Epiphanes, who
tried to impose pagan ways of life, thought, and worship on
them. The author of Daniel is trying to strengthen the
faith of his people, recalling their past triumphant stead-
fastness in the face of fierce persecution. For the author
of Daniel, the truth is that God always has been and
always will be with his people, but in illustrating this
truth, the author would not have used the same historical
method that is used today. The Hebrew reader would
ask, "What does the passage mean?" while we tend to ask
"Did these events really happen, and was it possible in
those days to increase furnace heat sevenfold?"

Palestine, although it was one of the smallest nations
in the empire, was also the most difficult for the Greek
and Roman colonizers to govern because the Jews were so
dedicated to the one God of Abraham, Isaac, and Jacob.
The Jews were justly proud of their own history and their
election as the chosen people, and they considered their
descent from Abraham to be their salvation. When Jesus
tells Abraham's descendants that their father is the Evil
One, Jesus is threatening their individual identity and

national security. It is not surprising that they want to stone him.

We need to reflect on this passage and pray to understand its implications. We cannot find salvation—or justification or right relationship with God, whatever words we use—simply by being of a particular race, nation, religion, or church. Yet it was the belief that salvation could be found only in Christianity that gave impetus to its missionary movement. As the churches divided, each claiming to be the true church, Christians persecuted and killed one another in good conscience, each convinced that they alone could offer salvation to all. This belief, although less prevalent today, still infects us, keeps us apart, weakens us, prevents cooperation, and leaves each church so intent on its own maintenance that it has little or no energy left for mission.

As human beings we possess the need to belong to a family, race, nation, group, or tradition. But because we are each unique and have a unique relationship with God and everyone and everything else in creation, we have a unique role to play in the world. Because we are free, it can never be enough for us to say, "I am saved because I belong to this church, this religious group," and so on. All these things are given to us to help us find God, but they are not God himself. It is right for us to appreciate, love, and be faithful to our own religious tradition, whatever it is, but we also have to test our own tradition and our understanding of it. Is it helping us to love God and our neighbor as we love ourselves?

Prayer

> God, we thank you for all your gifts: the gift of creation,
> of the Scriptures, of tradition, of the church. Help us to
> recognize you in your gifts without identifying you with
> them. We ask you this through Jesus Christ, our Lord.
> Amen.

Thursday

THE COVENANT

Genesis 17:3–9; Psalm 105; John 8:51–59

I will establish my Covenant between myself and you, and your descendants after you, generation after generation, a Covenant in perpetuity, to be your God and the God of your descendants after you. . . . You on your part shall maintain my Covenant, yourself and your descendants after you, generation after generation.

GEΠESİS 17:7, 9

[Jesus said to the Jews:] "I tell you most solemnly, whoever keeps my word will never see death." The Jews said, "Now we know for certain that you are possessed. Abraham is dead, and the prophets are dead, and yet you say, 'Whoever keeps my word will never know the taste of death.' Are you greater than our father Abraham, who is dead?" . . . Jesus replied: "I tell you most solemnly, before Abraham ever was, I Am." At this they picked up stones to throw at him.

JOHΠ 8:51—53, 58—59

Regardless of the Christian denomination to which we belong, we believe that we are children of the covenant, that the God of the Jewish people, of Abraham, Isaac, and Jacob, is also our God. The covenant with Abraham is God's covenant with us now, and on our part we pledge to maintain that covenant.

For Israel, maintaining the covenant meant mirroring God in all her dealings. Most of the Law outlines the way in which the Jews must mirror the compassion, tenderness, mercy, and justice of God, not only in their dealings with other Jews, but also with strangers.

Paul says of Jesus that "he is the image of the unseen God and the first-born of all creation, for in him were created all things in heaven and on earth: everything visible and everything invisible . . . all things were created through him and for him" (Colossians 1:15–16). Jesus is the full revelation of the covenant, the unbreakable bond between God and ourselves, for Jesus, a human like us, can say, "before Abraham ever was, I Am" (John 8:58). This is an astonishing claim, not only about Jesus of Nazareth but also about our own identity and destiny.

To believe in Jesus' divinity is to believe that he is the image of the unseen God and that in him all peoples, religious and nonreligious, are being called into unity with God, with one another, and with all creation. God's ways are not our ways, and his thoughts are not our thoughts (Isaiah 55:9). He works in every individual in ways that transcend our thinking and imagining so that there is no religion, nation, group, or individual from whom we cannot learn something, for that which is of God is in everyone.

Some Christians believe that interfaith relations are a danger to the Christian faith; others believe that interfaith relations are integral to the Christian faith. If we believe that Christ is, in Paul's words, the image of the unseen God, in whom all creation has its being and in whom all things in heaven and on earth are to be reconciled (Colossians 1:15–20), then this reconciliation must somehow include all people of all religions. This raises a question for Christians: can we ever claim to have a complete knowledge of Christ and of his ways? Paul says that the love of Christ goes "beyond all knowledge" (Ephesians 3:19).

All the Christians I have met who are engaged in interfaith work claim that their study and friendship with people of other religions has helped them appreciate in a new way the breadth and depth of their own faith. One striking example in my own experience was my friendship with Stella Reekie, a Church of Scotland deaconess who died in 1983. Having been appointed by Christian churches in Scotland to work with immigrants, she kept an open house, and people of many different religions came to see her. At her funeral, mourners included Sikhs, Hindus, Muslims, Baha'is, and Jews, as well as Christians of different denominations. The Sikh who gave the address ended his speech by saying, "I have never understood what Christians meant when they say, 'Jesus died for our sins,' but I know that Stella died for our sins." Stella was not a theologian, but her Christ-centered life was the very stuff of theology. God's ways are not our ways; his thoughts are not our thoughts. May he preserve us from trying to take over, because in doing so, we limit the ways of God and of his Christ to those patterns of thought and behavior with which we are familiar and of which we approve.

Prayer

God, give us the grace to wonder at our being and our calling to live in covenant with you, and help us to recognize you, Lord of all creation, in everyone we meet. We ask you this through Jesus Christ, our Lord. Amen.

Friday

OUR IDENTITY

*Jeremiah 20:10–13; Psalm 18;
John 10:31–42*

*All those who used to be my friends watched for my down-
fall, "Perhaps he will be seduced into error. Then we will
master him and take our revenge!" But Yahweh is at my
side, a mighty hero.*

JEREMIAH 20:10–11

*The Jews [said,] "We are not stoning you for doing a good
work but for blasphemy: you are only a man and you claim
to be God." Jesus answered: "Is it not written in your Law:
I said, you are gods? So the Law uses the word gods of those
to whom the word of God was addressed. . . . Yet you say to
someone the Father has consecrated and sent into the world,
'You are blaspheming,' because he says, 'I am the Son of
God.'"*

JOHN 10:33–36

In praying the Gospels imaginatively, many people find
that while they can imagine the scene as though it were

now happening, they can be present only as observers, not as participants. This reflects a truth of our lives, that while we may admire, be attracted by, and want to follow Christ and his teaching, we do so from a distance. We feel that he is ahead of us, not, as he is for Jeremiah, at our side. We may also feel that while it is all very well for Christ to preach and live what he preaches and to die so heroically and generously for us, he is God, after all, and thus has an unfair advantage.

In the fascinating book *The Trial of the Man Who Claimed to be God*, author Douglas Harding describes an imaginary trial that takes place in Britain after the blasphemy law has been changed as a result of the Salman Rushdie affair. The defendant is a Christian. The prosecution bring forward a large number and variety of witnesses. The defendant conducts his own defense but provides no living witnesses, only dead ones, wise and holy men and women from the past, both Christian and non-Christian. The book is a scholarly and entertaining study of a question we all have to ask ourselves: "Who am I?"

Remember my friend Donald, who, at a group meeting, wanted to say, "I am a unique manifestation of God" instead of give his occupation to describe himself? Why do we feel that we have to give our occupation when we introduce ourselves? It gives us a sense of security and assures us of our place on society's rung and thus of our worth, a custom that adds to the embarrassment of those who have no occupation.

Donald is a very wise man who stands in awe of no one and is not impressed by title or station. Measuring our own and other people's worth by occupation or title is subtly destructive of ourselves and of them, for it prevents us from appreciating who we and they really are. When we identify our worth by our possessions, achievements, or place in society, we tend to look down on those who have not reached our level, and if we lose any of these things, we feel that we count for nothing.

I once gave a retreat to a L'Arche assistant (L'Arche communities are made up of disabled persons and their helpers), who after eight years was trying to decide whether to make a permanent commitment to L'Arche and work with the mentally handicapped for the rest of her life. I asked her what she had gained from her last eight years. She said that she had joined L'Arche feeling that she had something to contribute—teacher qualifications and a good university degree. But the handicapped people with whom she worked were not at all impressed by her qualifications, and she felt devastated. The most valuable thing she had learned at L'Arche was that her worth was her own being, not her achievements, qualifications, or place in society. This is what is meant by "Blessed are the poor, theirs is the kingdom of heaven."

In prayer, hear God say to you, "I have called you by your name, you are mine. . . . You are precious in my eyes, because you are honored and I love you" (Isaiah 43:1, 4). And hear Jesus say to you, "I am the vine, you are the branches," "You and I are one undivided person." If we could really know this truth at the depths of our being, then we would have the most wonderful inner freedom. Catherine of Genoa, a sixteenth-century mystic, once said, "My God is me, nor do I recognize any other me, but God himself." Whether worried, anxious, and agitated or pleased and delighted, it is good to ask ourselves who is worried, anxious, and so on: is it God, or is it me?

Prayer

Open our eyes, Lord, to the wonder of our being. We were in your mind before the world was created and were formed to be one with Christ and live in love in your presence. We ask you this through Jesus Christ, our Lord. Amen.

Saturday

ONE MAN SHOULD DIE

Ezekiel 37:21–28; Psalm 40;
Jeremiah 31:10–13; John 11:45–57

I am going to take the sons of Israel from the nations. . . .
I shall gather them together from everywhere and bring
them home to their own soil. . . . I shall rescue them from
all the betrayals they have been guilty of; I shall cleanse
them; they shall be my people and I will be their God. . . .
And the nations will learn that I am Yahweh the sanctifier
of Israel, when my sanctuary is with them for ever.

EZEKİEL 37:21, 23, 28

Many of the Jews who had come to visit Mary and had
seen what [Jesus] did believed in him, but some of them
went to tell the Pharisees what Jesus had done. Then the
chief priests and Pharisees called a meeting. "Here is this
man working all these signs," they said, "and what action
are we taking? If we let him go . . . everybody will believe
in him, and the Romans will come and destroy the Holy
Place and our nation." One of them, Caiaphas, the high
priest that year, said, "You don't seem to have grasped the

situation at all; you fail to see that it is better for one man to die for the people, than for the whole nation to be destroyed." He did not speak in his own person, it was as high priest that he made this prophecy that Jesus was to die for the nation—and not for the nation only, but to gather together in unity the scattered children of God. From that day they were determined to kill him.

These two readings are in striking contrast. Through Ezekiel, God promises to bring unity and peace to the scattered Jewish nation, to cleanse them of all past betrayals, and to be their sanctifier and God, making them a sign for the nations. A few centuries later in the Gospel, the chief priests and the Pharisees, the legitimate authorities, are plotting to kill Jesus, the fulfillment of all God's promises. "If we let him go, everybody will believe in him, and the Romans will come and destroy the Holy Place and our nation," they say. Jesus is a threat to their national security, a point that Caiaphas sums up succinctly: "It is better for one man to die for the people, than for the whole nation to be destroyed." This advice has reverberated down the centuries. "Is it not better for a few hundred thousand to die in Dresden, Hiroshima, and Nagasaki than for our national security to be threatened?" "Is it not better for us to retain the power to annihilate millions than to risk the security and values of our nation?" The minds and hearts of today's authorities and chief priests have not changed except that they do not acknowledge Caiaphas's one-man limit.

We must pray to wake up—as individuals, as a church, and as a nation—to the truth that contemplating the suffering of Christ is not just commemorating a past event to make us feel religiously good. It is the unveiling of a

222 | SEVEN WEEKS FOR THE SOUL

present reality that makes us feel so uncomfortable that we have to radically change our ways.

"He did not speak in his own person, it was as high priest that he made this prophecy that Jesus was to die for the nation—and not for the nation only, but to gather together in unity the scattered children of God." Caiaphas spoke cynically and murderously. His statement may be compared to a false note that God, the master composer, takes and works into a new composition. Jesus' death will not only save the nation but will also gather in unity the scattered children of God.

God works through human sinfulness. The Jews present themselves in the Scriptures not as an exemplary people but as a stiff-necked generation, an unfaithful and treacherous people. It is God alone who bestows greatness upon them. As Belloc wrote, "How odd of God to choose the Jews." In the Gospels, two of the twelve betray him, and all desert him in the final crisis.

We need to apply these readings to our own lives. We contain the scattered children of Israel within ourselves, our base inclinations and desires, and our obstinate self-will and narrow vision, which is blinkered to our immediate self-interest, betraying our own deepest longings. Come before God with the scattered children and listen to him say, "I shall rescue you from all the betrayals you have been guilty of; I shall cleanse you; and I will be your God." Present to him the damage that has been done to you and the damage you have done, and beg him to take it all and work on it as he worked on Adam's and Caiaphas's sin. In this way the wrongs you have done may be transformed by his power into a source of blessing, not only for yourself and your peace but also for the peace of the world.

Prayer

God, deepen our trust in you, source of all goodness, and drive out from our hearts all servile fear, so that we may always direct our defiled hearts to you to be cleansed and transformed into channels of your love and mercy. We ask you this through Jesus Christ, our Lord. Amen.

Sunday

THE CROSS IN CHRISTIAN LIFE

*Isaiah 50:4–7; Psalm 22; Philippians
2:6–8; Matthew 26:14–27, 66*

*For my part, I made no resistance neither did I turn away.
I offered my back to those who struck me, my cheeks to
those who tore at my beard; I did not cover my face against
insult and spittle. The Lord Yahweh comes to my help, so
that I am untouched by the insults. So, too, I set my face
like flint; I know I shall not be shamed.*

ISAIAH 50:5–7

*His state was divine, yet he did not cling to his equality
with God but emptied himself to assume the condition of a
slave, and became as men are; and being as all men are, he
was humbler yet, even to accepting death, death on a cross.*

PHILIPPIANS 2:6–8

We read the Gospel account of Christ's passion not simply
to recall a past event but in order to recognize God in
the present.

Frequently, we hear "The Cross lies at the heart of Christian life" and "Unless we enter into the passion and death of Christ, we cannot share in his resurrection." The phrases are true, but in what sense is this "good news" to any except the masochists?

Some stories of saints' lives can leave the reader with the impression that the Christian journey is a kind of "sufferathon," with the person who suffers the most winning the gold. We are all afflicted with this false belief, and because we are told that suffering is a sign of God's favor, we can feel bad about feeling good. Some theologies of the cross do not help, suggesting a God who can only be appeased by the shedding of blood but is ready to accept the blood of his Son in place of the blood of us all. A theology of this nature can leave us feeling very grateful to Jesus but less keen on his heavenly Father. According to these beliefs, the most effective way for us to serve God would consist in our imposing the maximum suffering on ourselves and others.

Suffering in itself is an evil and should be avoided. While it is true that some people are ennobled by suffering, the majority are diminished or destroyed by it. God's will for us, as Scripture frequently says, is life, not destruction and death. Jesus did not will suffering; he prayed to escape from it: "Father, if it is possible, let this cup pass me by." He declared himself to be the fulfillment of Isaiah's prophecy: "The spirit of the Lord has been given to me, for he has anointed me. He has sent me to bring the good news to the poor, to proclaim liberty to captives and to the blind new sight, to set the downtrodden free" (Luke 4:18). It was because Jesus lived out this prophecy that he suffered, for he threatened those whose power, prosperity, and security depended on keeping the poor in their poverty and the downtrodden oppressed. If we let Christ be Christ in us, oppose injustice, and speak the truth in love, we will also suffer at the hands of those whose power we threaten, whether in church or state. To suffer in this way is to share in the passion of Christ. Keeping quiet in the face of injustice and oppression—doing nothing to oppose it—may be less painful, but it is also a refusal to enter into Christ's passion.

Much of our suffering has nothing to do with the cross of Christ, for it is not pain incurred through following him but that of our own bruised ego, which occurs when our own kingdom is threatened by criticism, loss of status, or financial loss. But if we can let God into this pain and show it to him, acknowledge its origin in our own egoism, and pray to be delivered from our own false securities, then the pain can become curative. It can lead us to freedom from our false attachments and to the knowledge that he really is our rock, refuge, and strength and that we have no other. Perhaps instead of trying to enter into the passion of Christ we should ask Christ to enter into our suffering, whether it is the suffering we endure through trying to follow him or the pain we feel when our own kingdom is threatened. It is in our own pain that we can find him present and beckoning. The Anima Christi is an ancient Latin prayer on the Passion. Here is a very free version of it:

Prayer

> *May thy mind and heart be mine,*
> *Thy body and blood heal mine,*
> *Thy blood act on me like wine.*
> *May the water from thy side cleanse me.*

In thy goodness always hear me.
Let thy wounds enfold me,
So that I become inseparable from thee.
From all that is evil protect me.
In life may I always hear thee;
In death may I see thee invite me
To be at one with all creation
In praise of thee and adoration.

Monday

LOVE AND MARKET FORCES

Isaiah 42:1–7; Psalm 27; John 12:1–11

⁷esus went to Bethany. . . . They gave a dinner for him
there; Martha waited on them and Lazarus was among
those at table. Mary brought in a pound of very costly
ointment, pure nard, and with it anointed the feet of
Jesus, wiping them with her hair; the house was full of the
scent of the ointment. Then Judas Iscariot—one of his
disciples, the man who was to betray him—said, "Why
wasn't this ointment sold for three hundred denarii, and
the money given to the poor?" He said this, not because he
cared about the poor, but because he was a thief; he was in
charge of the common fund and used to help himself to the
contributions. So Jesus said, "Leave her alone; she had to
keep this scent for the day of my burial. You have the poor
with you always, you will not always have me."

JOHN 12:1–8

The most quoted half-sentence from this Gospel passage
is "You have the poor with you always." It is used by those
who want to prove that concern with social reform, justice,

and peace is not a part of the essence of Christian faith. The essence of Christian faith is in this Gospel passage, but it is not in the phrase "You have the poor with you always."

You can pray imaginatively on the scene in the Gospel. See the room, the guests, the revived Lazarus, the industrious Martha. Mary, who had so annoyed Martha at a previous supper by sitting at Jesus' feet, is now engaged in another activity that does not help the cook and, as Judas points out, is also very wasteful.

Judas puts a price on everything. He would have been a model citizen today, when a balanced economy is the central political issue. Health care, housing, education, and social welfare are all regulated by the money available. As we have seen in society today, when economic principles are considered to be as absolute as the law of gravity, subjection to these principles is inevitable. The fallacy is in assuming that economic principles are absolute: they are not. Our economic laws and principles are a reflection of our values, and our values come from our hearts. "For where your treasure is, there will your heart be also" (Matthew 6:21). If our treasure is in the balance of payments, then our hearts will be there also: all things and all people will finally be controlled by their price. Market forces will rule, and as Scripture says, "the man who has will be given more; from the man who has not, even what he has will be taken away" (Mark 4:25).

In the Gospel passage, Mary is blissfully unaware of market forces as she pours expensive ointment over Jesus' feet and wipes them with her hair, expressing a love beyond price. In Mark's account of the anointing, Jesus says, "She has anointed my body beforehand for its burial. I tell you solemnly, wherever throughout all the world the Good

News is proclaimed, what she has done will be told also, in remembrance of her."

We need to ponder this passage and let the beauty of Mary's gesture touch the depths of our hearts, where love dwells, the same love Mary surrendered to and expressed by anointing Jesus' feet. "Before the world was made, he chose us, chose us in Christ . . . to live through love in his presence" (Ephesians 1:4). Mary has found herself, a self that is absorbed in Jesus, so she prepares him for his burial. "God is love" (1 John 4:8).

It is easy for us to become so absorbed in surviving each day that we live outside of our lives, relating to others and to ourselves in a robotic fashion and missing the mystery of love, which is the heart of all life. A social welfare program could be successful in that it ensured every adult a sufficiency of necessities as well as a little extra for luxuries, such as expensive ointments, but if it was without love, it would create a hell on earth.

"That is why I am telling you not to worry about your life and what you are to eat, nor about your body and how you are to clothe it. . . . No; set your hearts on his kingdom, and these other things will be given you as well" (Luke 12:22, 31). God's love will prompt us to care for one another as we care for ourselves. We will then discover a new understanding of the meaning of a balance of payments and that very different economic laws exist, laws that spring from our hearts and bring life, instead of laws that wither our hearts by forcing us, like Judas, to put a price on everything.

Prayer

> *We thank you, God, for the love that created us and for that with which you draw us to yourself. May the Spirit who prompted Mary to perform her extravagant gesture inform our lives, driving out every form of price-reckoning stinginess. We ask you this through Jesus Christ, our Lord. Amen.*

Tuesday

PETER'S DENIAL

*Isaiah 49:1–6; Psalm 71;
John 13:21–33, 36–38*

*Simon Peter said, "Lord, where are you going?" Jesus
replied, "Where I am going you cannot follow me now; you
will follow me later." Peter said to him, "Why can't I follow
you now? I will lay down my life for you." "Lay down your
life for me?" answered Jesus. "I tell you most solemnly, before
the cock crows you will have disowned me three times."*

JOHN 13:36–38

We read the Scriptures about God's dealing with Israel in
the past in order to recognize God at work in our present
circumstances. In the Gospel accounts of the Passion, we
see how God, through Jesus, enters into human suffering,
disillusionment, betrayal, and death. There is no depth of
human suffering where God is present in the depths of all
human suffering. We cannot enter into the sufferings of
Jesus until we enter into our own experience of pain and
suffering, for we meet him not in his suffering of two
thousand years ago but in the pain of our own lives now.

Both today's and tomorrow's Gospel readings describe the betrayal of Judas, but today's reading also includes Peter's betrayal, so we will leave our reflection on Judas's betrayal until tomorrow.

When Peter said, "I will lay down my life for you," he was being totally sincere. Jesus' reply—"I tell you most solemnly, before the cock crows you will have disowned me three times"—must have devastated Peter because Peter's own conscious mind was so full of loyalty that he could not accept the possibility of his ever denying Jesus.

"The word of God . . . cuts like any double-edged sword but more finely: it can slip through the place where the soul is divided from the spirit, or joints from the marrow" (Hebrews 4:12). We can look at Peter's denial as an event that happened to Peter two thousand years ago, a regrettable event at the time but one that had a happy ending for Peter and for us because it assures us of the possibility of forgiveness, even if we fail like Peter. While we consider this, a little voice inside of us is telling us that we would never be capable of failing as Peter failed. If we hear such a voice, we need to pray for enlightenment so that we can know the falsity of the voice, because we are no better than Peter and probably a great deal worse.

In contemplating the passage imaginatively, without forcing anything, we can pray to be taken into the event, where we can hear the words of Jesus being spoken to us. When Peter sincerely professes his loyalty, it is as though Jesus replies: "Don't make pompous assertions about laying down your life. You don't have enough of a hold on your own life to lay it down for anyone. If you were to try to take hold of it, it would run through your fingers like sand. In fact, you are a nonperson." Can we think of anything more devastating than to hear Jesus speak these words to us in response to our plea of "I want to know, love, and serve you"? Could he say anything more cruel and destructive?

It has been only recently that the books of the Bible have been broken up into chapters. The final words of today's Gospel reading are the final words of John 13. John 14 begins with Jesus' further comment: "Trust in God still, and trust in me." John never puts sentences together at random: each is carefully and deliberately placed. The devastating comment Jesus makes to Peter and to us can plunge us into the depths of despair, but the verse that follows reveals the deeper truth of things. The despair we feel is based on a false assumption, namely that the truth about us rests in ourselves: in our integrity, strength of character, and reliability. What Jesus reveals— and it is the revelation of the whole Bible—is that God, not ourselves, is our rock, refuge, and strength, our light and our salvation: there is no other.

God is always greater, greater than our sins and defects. For those who suffer from a sense of lingering guilt, whether from specific sins or a general sense of unidentifiable guilt, from scruples or a sense of worth-lessness, it is good to acknowledge the guilty feelings and then hear these words spoken to you, "Trust in God still, and trust in me."

God is in every situation, even the most desperate, leading us as he led Peter to a knowledge of our true selves, and we can find ourselves only when we lose ourselves in his self. "Anyone who loses his life for my sake, that man will save it" (Luke 9:24).

Prayer

O God, give me the courage to listen and reflect on my fears and doubts and the grace to hear you say to my soul, "Don't be afraid, for I am always with you, your rock, refuge, and strength." We ask you this through Jesus Christ, our Lord. Amen.

Wednesday

JUDAS'S BETRAYAL

Isaiah 50:4–9; Psalm 69;
Matthew 26:14–26

When evening came he was at table with the twelve disciples. And while they were eating he said, "I tell you solemnly, one of you is about to betray me." They were greatly distressed and started asking him in turn, "Not I, Lord, surely?" He answered, "Someone, who has dipped his hand into the dish with me, will betray me. The Son of Man is going to his fate, as the scriptures say he will, but alas for that man by whom the Son of Man is betrayed! Better for that man if he had never been born!" Judas, who was to betray him, asked in his turn, "Not I, Rabbi, surely?" "They are your own words," answered Jesus.

MATTHEW 26:20–25

When Ignatius of Loyola comes to consider the passion of Christ in his *Spiritual Exercises*, he suggests that in looking at the Passion, we should see "how much Jesus suffers in his humanity." This is an important reminder because the teaching we have been given and the preaching we have heard can sometimes leave us with a glorified picture of Jesus, mostly divine and scarcely human. Some have taught that during his life Jesus lived constantly conscious of the beatific vision, in a state of total bliss with a clear knowledge of the future. Such an interpretation leads us to imagine Jesus choosing eleven apostles and then looking around for some shifty-eyed character to make up the total, "that the Scriptures might be fulfilled."

Jesus, image of the unseen God, was a human being with human limitations, a human consciousness, and a human unconscious. He had to grow and learn. "And Jesus increased in wisdom, in stature, and in favor with God and men" (Luke 2:52).

Jesus must have loved Judas and known him intimately, choosing him in good faith. We cannot know the human consciousness of Jesus or of anyone else with certainty: we can only conjecture. My conjecture is that Judas's betrayal was for Jesus one of the most hurtful incidents in his passion, for those closest to us inflict the greatest pain. Jesus must have prayed for Judas after Judas's betrayal and included Judas in his prayer on the cross: "Father, forgive them for they know not what they do."

Judas was so immersed in his own vision for the future that when his friendship with Jesus seemed to him a hindrance, he dropped Jesus. To Judas's credit, he soon came to realize the enormity of his crime.

We are all capable of Judas-like betrayal, so convinced of the righteousness of our cause that we do not give a second thought to its victims, or even if we do give them a second thought, we remain convinced of the rightness of our action. In the past, Britain as a nation was able to unleash destruction on its enemies, killing far more innocent civilians than armed combatants and justifying the action in the name of patriotism. Today, Britain's defense system includes four Trident submarines, any one of which contains many times the firepower of the total firepower used in World War II. The cause is a good one: the defense of our nation; the means used are demonic.

If this last paragraph seems exaggerated, ask yourself, "Who is Christ; where do I meet him, and what is the connection between his passion and death and our life now?" To believe in his divinity is to believe that he lives in every individual and that what we do to another we also do to him.

The danger of being dedicated to a cause that leads us to disregard others is written large in our national defense policies, but the same danger is also present in all our activities. In politics, industry, business, and the professions, people can be treated as things, useful insofar as they promote the enterprise and disposable when they cease to be of use. In the church too, in the name of Christ's kingdom, people can be similarly treated. The nobility of the cause makes the abuse of individuals all the more scandalous. Obviously, people have to move on, leave jobs and positions, but it is the way in which this is done that marks the difference between the kingdom of God and that of mammon. God's kingdom is a kingdom of attitudes, not of religious boundaries.

With Peter's denial and Judas's betrayal, we need to beg God to alert us to our own "thingifying" tendencies that occur whenever our enthusiasm for a cause, no matter how good or religious in itself, leads us to use other people to their own detriment or to discount, despise, and discard them.

Prayer

O God, may our contemplation of your passion and death so affect the core of our minds and hearts that all our desires, decisions, and actions may be directed to your kingdom of justice, peace, and truth. We ask you this through Jesus Christ, our Lord. Amen.

Thursday

THE WASHING OF FEET

Exodus 12:1–8, 11–14;
1 Corinthians 11:23–26; John 13:1–15

For this is what I received from the Lord, and in turn
passed on to you: that on the same night that he was
betrayed, the Lord Jesus took some bread, and thanked God
for it and broke it, and he said, "This is my body, which is
for you; do this as a memorial of me." In the same way he
took the cup after supper, and said, "This cup is the new
covenant in my blood. Whenever you drink it, do this as a
memorial of me."

1 CORINTHIANS 11:23–25

Jesus knew that the Father had put everything into his
hands, and that he had come from God and was returning
to God, and he got up from table, removed his outer garment
and, taking a towel, wrapped it around his waist; he then
poured water into a basin and began to wash the disciples'
feet and to wipe them with the towel he was wearing.

He came to Simon Peter, who said to him, "Lord, are
you going to wash my feet?" Jesus answered, "At the moment

you do not know what I am doing, but later you will understand." "Never!" said Peter. "You shall never wash my feet." Jesus replied, "If I do not wash you, you can have nothing in common with me."... When he had washed their feet and put on his clothes again he went back to the table. "Do you understand," he said, "what I have done to you? You call me Master and Lord, and rightly; so I am. If I, then, the Lord and Master, have washed your feet, you should wash each other's feet."

JOHП 13:3–8, 12–14

In some parts of the early church, the washing of feet was celebrated as a sacrament, and still today some churches practice a ceremony of foot washing on Maundy Thursday.

At first reading, it seems strange that John's description of the Last Supper would omit the institution of the Eucharist, the central theme of the other Gospel accounts. But in contemplating this passage, we can begin to see that the washing of feet and the breaking of bread both signify the same reality, namely that in Jesus, "the bread of life," God is giving himself to us. "If I do not wash you, you can have nothing in common with me."

The ritual of foot washing annoys many Christians, who feel that it is farcical for domineering clergy members to pretend they are servants. The Gospel accounts of the Last Supper can be reassuring for those who are irked by clerical domination. The Gospels describe at length not only the treachery of Judas and the betrayal of Peter but also, in Luke's version, the argument in which the apostles engaged, after they received the Eucharist, over who was the greatest among them. So Jesus understands the problem.

John prefaces his description with "Jesus knew that the Father had put everything into his hands." Knowing this,

Jesus takes the towel and begins to wash the apostles' feet. This is a revelation of God in Jesus, a God who serves. Unless we experience him as a God who serves, we have nothing in common with him.

At the end of his *Spiritual Exercises*, Ignatius offers an exercise called "Contemplation to attain the love of God." It includes the suggestion "Consider how God works and labors for me in all creatures upon the face of the earth, how he conducts himself as one who labors. Thus, in the heavens, the elements, the plants, the fruits, the cattle . . . he gives being, conserves them, confers life and sensation."

Imagine yourself at the Last Supper and let Jesus wash your feet. What does he say to you as he works? "You should have cleaned them properly and put on a clean pair of socks before coming to me"? Does he show distaste as he removes the dirt, point out the deformities, blame us for our foot care failures, and move on to more respectable feet? Or does he hold our feet as though they are precious, wash them gently and with compassion, smile at you as he washes, and apparently enjoy what he is doing? Hear him say to you when he is finished, "Care for those around you as I have cared for you."

Prayer

> *In all that I experience, Lord, help me to recognize you laboring for me, so that filled with gratitude, I may act toward others with the generosity you show to me. I ask you this through Jesus Christ, our Lord. Amen.*

Friday

THE DEATH OF JESUS

Isaiah 52:13–53:12; Psalm 31;
John 18:1–19:42

Yet he was pierced through for our faults, crushed for our sins. On him lies a punishment that brings us peace, and through his wounds we are healed. . . . By his sufferings shall my servant justify many, taking their faults on himself. . . . He was bearing the faults of many and praying all the time for sinners.

ISAİAH 53:5, II—I2

"So you are a king then?" said Pilate. "It is you who say it," answered Jesus. "Yes, I am a king. I was born for this, I came into the world for this: to bear witness to the truth; and all who are on the side of truth listen to my voice." . . . The chief priests answered, "We have no king except Caesar." . . . When they came to Jesus, they found he was already dead, and so instead of breaking his legs one of the soldiers pierced his side with a lance; and immediately there came out blood and water.

JOHП 18:37; 19:16, 33—34

There is a place and time for thinking about the Passion, for reading commentaries and theorizing about its meaning. But today we are going to be still, standing in imagination in the event and begging God to lead us into the mystery of his love. The death of Jesus was a historic, once-for-all event, but the love of God that expressed itself in this event is the love in which we now live and move.

How can we say that God is good when we look at the horrors of human life? Natural disasters, animals preying on one another, and the built-in destructive viruses that bring disease and death are all bad enough, but human minds and hearts are the most destructive forces in nature, capable of annihilating all life on our planet. Can we be honest with ourselves and still say, "God is good"?

Reason, philosophies, and theologies can only scratch the surface of the problem of evil. The mystery of Christ's passion and death upsets all our theories. If God is "the supreme Spirit who alone exists of himself and is infinite in all perfections," "the First Mover," and "the Uncaused Cause," then is he not ultimately responsible for the existence of evil?

Jesus reveals a most surprising God: "God's foolishness is wiser than human wisdom, and God's weakness is stronger than human strength" (1 Corinthians 1:25). God, in Jesus, refuses to exercise power as we understand it, identifies himself with every human being, empties "himself to assume the condition of a slave" (Philippians 2:7), and is a powerless, silent, and hidden God who enters into the pain, weakness, sinfulness, and corruption of human life. God, in Jesus, absorbs the concentrated and venomous onslaught of sin and transforms it. On the cross he prays, "Father, forgive them; they do not know what they are doing" (Luke 23:34). John expresses the transformation with "When they came to Jesus, they found he was already dead, and so instead of breaking his legs one of the soldiers pierced his side with a lance; and immediately there came out blood and water" (John 19:33–34).

If Jesus has suffered for us, why do we still have to suffer the effects of our own and other people's sinfulness? We suffer because if we are to be healed and at one with God in his work of transformation, we have to enter with him the pain of things. It is in our woundedness, not in our power, that we find him. God weeps in our hearts, but his tears are healing tears, springs of everlasting life, cleansing us, sustaining us, transforming us, giving us hope when everything seems hopeless, and assuring us that even in all our bewilderment, uncertainty, disillusionment, and ignorance, "All manner of things shall be well" (Mother Julian). Love is always in the tears of things— invincible but hidden, apparently powerless, yet reconciling all that is in heaven and all that is on earth (Colossians 1:20).

Prayer

> *God, in the sufferings and death of Christ, from whose side there came the blood and water, you are showing us your love. Open our eyes so that we can recognize your love and accept it in every event of our lives. We ask you this through Jesus Christ, our Lord. Amen.*

Saturday

JESUS IN THE TOMB

Wisdom 3:1–9; Psalm 143; John 19:38–42

But the souls of the virtuous are in the hands of God, no torment shall ever touch them. In the eyes of the unwise, they did appear to die, their going looked like a disaster, their leaving us, like annihilation; but they are in peace.

WISDOM 3:1–3

After this, Joseph of Arimathaea, who was a disciple of Jesus—though a secret one because he was afraid of the Jews—asked Pilate to let him remove the body of Jesus. Pilate gave permission, so they came and took it away. Nicodemus came as well—the same one who had first come to Jesus at nighttime—and he brought a mixture of myrrh and aloes, weighing about a hundred pounds. They took the body of Jesus and wrapped it with the spices in linen cloths, following the Jewish burial custom. At the place where he had been crucified there was a garden, and in this garden a new tomb in which no one had yet been buried. Since it was the Jewish Day of Preparation and the tomb was near at hand, they laid Jesus there.

JOHN 19:38–42

It is good for us to reflect on Jesus being laid in the tomb after his death on the first Good Friday. As we contemplate Jesus dead in the tomb, the reality of his death and of our own will sink more deeply into our consciousness.

In imagination, see yourself with the dead Jesus, perhaps as he is depicted in Michelangelo's *Pieta*, in the arms of Mary. Gaze upon him as though you were present in the tomb. See his face in death and the wounds of his body and speak to God as your heart prompts you.

> When we were baptized we went into the tomb
> with him and joined him in death, so that as Christ
> was raised from the dead by the Father's glory, we
> too might live a new life.
>
> ROMANS 6:4

Because we know that Jesus will rise again, we may tend to skip over the fact of his death and the tragedy of it, spend Holy Saturday in a state of religious inertia, and then find that our inner state remains inert and unable to experience the joy of Easter.

A young and wonderfully gifted man, who can draw together sworn enemies among his own people and bring a message of hope for all—men and women, Jews and Greeks, Barbarians and Scythians—is sentenced to the most brutal death in the name of religion, law, and order. He possesses clarity of mind and tenderness of heart and reveals a God who liberates the downtrodden, brings good news to the poor, gives sight to the blind, identifies himself with every human being, and tells us to love our enemies.

He was a man of vision, of dreams and enthusiasm: "I have come to bring fire to the earth, and how I wish it were blazing already! There is a baptism I must still receive, and how great is my distress till it is over!" (Luke 12:49–50). Did he feel a sense of total failure as he hung on the cross or experience disillusionment and hopelessness as he found himself condemned by the religious authorities to which he, as a Jew, was subject? Was his cry on the cross, "My God, my God, why have you forsaken me?" simply an excerpt from a psalm he happened to be praying, or was it a cry from the depths of his being?

For the believer no pain is worse than the pain of feeling abandoned by God. God, in Jesus, meets us in the depths of our suffering, in our sense of total hopelessness, failure, and abandonment. We need to ponder this truth and pray to know the presence of God in the depths of our being, at a level beyond our conscious minds and feelings. God is always greater than our sinfulness, failures, and feelings of disillusionment and despair.

Our consciousness, as we have seen, seems to consist of layers, and our inner journey is a journey through those layers, through deaths and resurrections to, in the words of Newman's Gerontius, "that strange and uttermost collapse of all that makes me man." Today, it is good for us to think on our own death while praying to know that in that moment of uttermost collapse we will know the truth of things, that God is our rock, our refuge, our life, and our salvation.

Prayer

> *God, you have poured your Spirit, who lived in Jesus and raised him from the dead, into our hearts. May his Spirit Easter in us, bringing us his peace to sustain us in*

*our conflicts and his joy to strengthen us in our weakness,
and may his love for you and all creation invade our
minds and hearts. We ask you this through Jesus Christ,
our Lord. Amen.*

The Day of Resurrection

CHRIST IS RISEN, ALLELUIA!

Acts 10:34–43; Psalm 118; John 20:1–9

> *So Peter set out with the other disciple to go to the tomb.*
> *They ran together, but the other disciple, running faster*
> *than Peter, reached the tomb first; he bent down and saw the*
> *linen cloths lying on the ground, but did not go in. Simon*
> *Peter who was following now came up, went right into the*
> *tomb, saw the linen cloths on the ground, and also the cloth*
> *that had been over his head; this was not with the linen*
> *cloths but rolled up in a place by itself. Then the other disci-*
> *ple who had reached the tomb first also went in; he saw and*
> *he believed. Till this moment they had failed to understand*
> *the teaching of scripture, that he must rise from the dead.*
>
> JOHN 20:3—9

We have been on this journey now for seven weeks and have finally reached the day of resurrection. Yet in one sense, nothing has changed. If we focus on this scene, it can seem anticlimactic. I still have the same temperament as I did on the day I started this journey. I still bear the same wounds, inflicted by others and by myself; I probably still live in the same place with the same people; I probably still have the same job, or lack of one, and the same problems to face.

Faith does not change the external world, but it changes the way in which we perceive it, and it is from this change in our perception that external change happens.

In today's Gospel, Peter and John run to the tomb. John gets there first but hesitates outside. Peter rushes straight in, and John then follows. "He saw and he believed." John saw an empty tomb, a scene of desolation: he believed Jesus was risen.

The word *belief* in English connotes gullibility, acceptance without proof. *Belief* in the New Testament means much more than the English word can convey. Belief is knowing, but a knowing that is not based solely on observation, inner reasoning, logical deduction, or the assurance of other people. Belief is an inner sensing, more like intuition. We cannot create it or force ourselves into it; all we can do is be still and discover the gift within ourselves. "The Spirit of him who raised Jesus from the dead is living in you" (Romans 8:11). This is the reality in which we live. By praying the Gospel scenes imaginatively, we can now meet the risen Christ, the pledge of our resurrection, living within us and among us.

But how reliable are the Gospel accounts? Was there really an empty tomb? Did Jesus really rise again from the dead? What kind of body did he have? Does life after death really exist? If so, what kind of body will we have?

These are all very interesting and important questions, but if we try to answer these questions before we pray the resurrection scenes, we will never get started. Accept the resurrection narratives as they are presented in the Gospels, leaving these other questions aside for the moment. This is not intellectual dishonesty but intellectual humility, an acknowledgment that the Resurrection is a mystery into which God alone can lead us and in which we are now living. Stand with John in the empty tomb and pray to believe as he believed. Be with the other disciples in the upper room, listen to their fears, and tell them of your own. See the risen Christ among you and hear him say to you, "Peace," as he shows you his wounded hands and side. Imagination can put us in touch with the reality that Christ is risen and is our peace. Be with Mary in the garden, recognizing him in the gardener. Be with the two disciples on the road to Emmaus and meet him in the stranger. Be still and hear his Spirit in your heart calling you by name and saying, "I am closer to you than you are to yourself. I shall never leave you, for you and I are one undivided person."

Then bring your attention back into the present and look around.

> With the drawing of this Love and the voice of
>   this Calling
> We shall not cease from exploration
> And the end of all our exploring
> Will be to arrive where we started
> And know the place for the first time.
>
> T. S. ELIOT

The Lord is truly risen, is within us and among us. Alleluia!

Additional Notes for Group Meetings

First Meeting
(after Week One)

How you conduct this first meeting depends on the nature of your group. If you are strangers to one another, the first meeting can most usefully be spent in becoming acquainted. The more at ease you become with each other, the more likely it will be that you will be able to share your prayer experiences later. The deeper layers of consciousness where change occurs can be touched only when there is an atmosphere of trust.

If these meetings are to be helpful, it is essential that members treat whatever is shared in the group as confidential. Confidentiality in this context means that members pledge not to reveal any part of an individual's contributions that they would not want to reveal if that individual were present.

If you are strangers to each other, it can be useful to start the meeting by chatting in pairs. A useful talking point might be "What are you hoping to gain from these meetings?"

Having chatted in pairs, introduce the person you have been talking with to the whole group. Then someone might want to give a brief summary of the notes presented in the introduction on the purpose and method of conducting your meetings and invite comment. This may take you the rest of the meeting, but before you finish, address these practical issues:

- Arrange the time and place of your next meeting.

- Appoint a different chairperson for each meeting, and confirm arrangements for the next one.

- Invite the group to reflect during the coming week on their own faith journeys (described in chapter 5).

- End the meeting with a few minutes of silent prayer for each other.

If you do know each other, you could start your meeting by briefly summarizing the notes in the introduction and inviting comment from the group. Then introduce the idea of our own individual faith journeys. We read the Bible to help us recognize the God of Abraham, Isaac, and Jacob, the Father of our Lord, Jesus Christ, at work in our own lives, so it is important to be in touch with our own history.

When you begin to share, take a few moments of silence after anyone speaks. The silence serves a double purpose: it is a mark of respect for the speaker, and it also allows what he or she has said to sink more deeply into your consciousness. This sharing is a listening exercise, so don't judge or analyze what anyone says, still less attempt to sort it out. You may respond to each other if someone's story touches on your experience, but remember that you are sharing life experiences, not theories.

This sharing of faith journeys may take several meetings, but it is time well spent. You are looking at your life journeys and listening to the action of God now in your group, the same God who brought Israel out of Egypt, through the wilderness, and into the Promised Land.

It might be wise to put a time limit of thirty minutes on any individual contribution. I once took part in a faith-sharing group in which the first speaker took ten minutes, the second speaker took twenty minutes, and the final speaker took two one-and-a-half-hour sessions!

Second Meeting (after Week Two)

If your group was unable to meet after the first week, take a look at the notes on group meetings in the introduction and also at the notes given for the first meeting at the beginning of this section.

If this is your second meeting, then start, or continue, the faith-journey sharing. Try to ensure that people will have about half an hour at the end of the meeting to comment on their experience of praying the readings during the week.

Whether you are relating your faith journey or commenting on your prayer during the week, try to speak from your gut rather than your head so that you are expressing your felt experience rather than presenting ideas or raising questions that have come out of the readings.

Having expressed your own felt experience in prayer, it is good to ask yourself what it was that occasioned those feelings. Was it a word, phrase, image, or memory? Whatever occasions a felt experience in us is usually more important than we realize at the time, so it is good to return to such words or images in later prayer periods. Felt experience in prayer or out of prayer is never boring to listen to because it achieves a communication deeper than words.

In listening to others too, listen with your gut rather than with your head. This means that instead of trying to remember the details of what each person in the group says you notice any feelings you experience when someone else is speaking. After the meeting is over, reflect on those feelings. They can usually tell us volumes about ourselves if only we can listen to them.

For example, I may begin to feel bored when a member of my group is speaking. This may be because the speaker is not speaking from his or her own felt experience but is chattering on in endless detail about something that has nothing to do with his or her felt experience. In this way my boredom may be justified. But on the other hand, I may be bored because I am so intent on what I want to say that I have no interest in anyone else's experience.

You will be tempted to try to analyze what you hear or to give advice. Resist the temptation and just listen. The best advice any of us can receive is the advice that comes to us from within our own psyche, the advice we discover for ourselves. Good listeners help this advice to surface in our minds. Bad listeners, who try to solve our problems and give us sound advice, prevent us from discovering advice for ourselves.

Before the end of this week's meeting, take a brief look at the Review of the Day prayer given on page 83. At a future meeting it would be worthwhile to exchange your experiences of praying in this way. Reviewing your day is an excellent way to get your bearings on your day-to-day journey.

At the end of the meeting, take a few minutes to pray silently for each other.

Third Meeting
(after Week Three)

If you are still listening to each other's faith journeys, then continue as last week, again leaving half an hour at the end of the meeting to share your felt experience in prayer during the week.

If you are finished with the faith journeys, you might want to talk with one another about your experience of trying the Review of the Day prayer. Have you found it helpful? In what ways?

As in last week's meeting, set aside at least half an hour at the end of this week's meeting so you can share your prayer experience of the past week, not only within your prayer time but also during the day. Often prayer is like an X ray. We may feel very little at the time, but our day will feel lighter, and we will feel less anxious, more interested, and alive.

Before the end of the meeting, invite each other to review chapter 4, "Finding Direction through Prayer," for next week.

End as usual with a few minutes of silent prayer.

Fourth Meeting
(after Week Four)

If you are still exchanging faith journeys, then continue as last week and leave commenting on the Review of the Day prayer and chapter 4 until later meetings.

Having read chapter 4, ask yourselves how far the guidelines for discernment correspond to your own experience. Can you recall any experience in your life that you could identify as consolation/desolation? If you were writing your own guidelines on discernment, what changes would you make to chapter 4?

If you pose these questions to one another in the group, avoid trying to satisfy your own curiosity, and instead try to make sure that your questions are enabling the person to explore his or her own experience. Remember to refrain from trying to solve one another's problems and speak always from your own experience.

End the meeting with a period of silent prayer.

FIFTH MEETING (AFTER WEEK FIVE)

If you have finished exchanging your faith journeys and have talked together about the Review of the Day prayer and the content of chapter 4, then concentrate on listening to each other's prayer experience during the past week. Do the guidelines given in chapter 4 illuminate anything you have experienced in your prayer during this week?

If you have found that on a particular day the prayer either attracted you to God or left you with a distaste for prayer, then it is important to return to those moments in subsequent prayer periods. Don't look at each day's readings and reflections as though they are a syllabus that you have to get through. If you can pray all week on the same Scripture passage, or even on the same phrase or word, then be content to do so. In his introduction to the *Spiritual Exercises*, Ignatius tells the retreat giver to always be brief in giving explanations to a retreatant, adding that it is not much knowledge that fills and satisfies the soul but the intimate understanding and relish of the truth.

Before your meeting ends, draw attention to chapter 1, especially the section dealing with the split nature of our spirituality, a subject on which you may like to reflect next week.

End the meeting with a period of silent prayer.

Sixth Meeting
(after Week Six)

Begin this week's meeting by listening to each other's prayer experience during the past week.

Having listened to each other, reflect on chapter 1, especially the section on the split nature of our spirituality. Do you agree that our spirituality is split? Has your prayer during these past weeks helped you in any way to find God more easily in the ordinary events of life?

If we are letting God be God in us and through us, one result will be a growing sense of compassion for the sufferings of people around us. Within your own immediate area, who are the people in need? What is being done to meet their needs? Is there any simple action that you could take or initiate as a group to meet any one of those needs? You might want to have your period of silent prayer before you discuss this question. Pray for guidance in identifying the needs of others and to know if God is prompting you, whether individually or as a group, to take the first step in responding to these needs.

Before the end of the meeting, decide whether you want to spend your last meeting on a review of the past seven weeks. Regardless of your decision, it is useful to do such a review individually. Try to find a word or phrase and an image that sum up the experience for you.

Seventh Meeting
(after Week Seven)

Listen as usual to each other's prayer experience during the past week, but set aside at least thirty minutes at the end of your meeting to review the past few weeks together.

Have you found a word or phrase and an image that expresses the period for you?

What have you found helpful in the group meetings?

Does what you have discovered during these past seven weeks have anything to do with your life in the weeks and months that lie ahead?

If you had to offer guidelines to a group, what suggestions would you make?

Do all, or some of you, want to continue to meet occasionally?

As the Quakers say, there is "that which is of God in everyone." Therefore we can bless one another, praying that each other's "hidden self" may "grow strong, so that Christ may live in your hearts through faith" (Ephesians 3:16–17). Sit silently in a circle, and let one of you get up and lay hands on the head of the person to his or her left. After that person has been blessed, then he or she will follow, blessing the person on his or her left, and so on, so that each person gives and receives a blessing. This is a good way of saying good-bye at the end of a series of group meetings.